What People Are Saying About

BREAKTHROUGH ENTREPRENEURSHIP

"This is *Seven Habits for Highly Effective Entrepreneurs*. If you want to succeed in business, read *Breakthrough Entrepreneurship*."

Ray Bingham
Managing Director, General Atlantic Partners

"Highly recommended reading for both students and professionals. A compelling guide for anyone who wants to become a successful entrepreneur or just think like one."

Tom Byers
Professor, Stanford University
Director, Stanford Technology Venture Partners

"This book tells you how to start a successful business and make a billion dollars. Even more, it is a book about how everyone in business should plan for success in our rapidly changing world. Give yourself a chance to be one of the successful new business leaders and *read this book*."

Jim Davidson
Co-CEO and Co-Founder, Silver Lake Partners

"*Breakthrough Entrepreneurship* captures the essence of entrepreneurship. This book provides plenty of practical advice for a new venture founder. It covers all the key concepts in crystal-clear terms, and illustrates them with compelling case studies."

Thomas Eisenmann
Professor, Harvard Business School
Former Co-Head, Media & Entertainment Practice, McKinsey & Co.

"Burgstone and Murphy provide a step-by-step guide for developing innovative ideas and turning them into booming businesses. The book is brimming with memorable examples and insights from some of the most successful entrepreneurs on the planet, including Burgstone himself. No would-be entrepreneur should be without this book."

Randall Kroszner
Professor, Booth School of Business, University of Chicago
Former Governor, United States Federal Reserve

"Entertaining and essential, *Breakthrough Entrepreneurship* is a must-read for anyone who dreams of coming up with a game-changing innovative idea, breaking away from the pack with that idea, and ultimately building a successful entrepreneurial venture."

Jay Light
Dean Emeritus, Harvard Business School

"From his early entrepreneurial days in his business school apartment, Jon Burgstone has had the insight to identify opportunities that others missed, the courage to pursue those opportunities, and the discipline to make it all happen. Together with Murphy in this new book, he provides a step-by-step framework to help others identify, pursue and succeed with their own start-up dreams."

Brad Loftus
Partner & Managing Director, The Boston Consulting Group

"*Breakthrough Entrepreneurship* isn't just a how-to guide. It's a step-by-step framework that shows you how to come up with great entrepreneurial ideas, build companies, make money, and lead a fulfilling life."

John Scharffenberger
Founder, Scharffenberger Cellars
Founder, Scharffen Berger Chocolate

"Entrepreneurs learn by doing, and *Breakthrough Entrepreneurship* is a great guide for all those who aspire to control their own destiny."

K. Ram Shriram
Founding Board Member, Google Inc.

"*Breakthrough Entrepreneurship* provides a comprehensive framework for entrepreneurial achievement, one drawn from the hands-on experience of some of America's most solid and successful company founders."

Ikhlaq Sidhu
Chief Scientist, Fung Institute
University of California, Berkeley

"Amazing and flat-out fun, *Breakthrough Entrepreneurship* is a must-read for anyone who dreams of finding true entrepreneurial success."

Matt Szulik
Ernst & Young
National Entrepreneur of the Year Award Winner

"*Breakthrough Entrepreneurship* tells readers everything they've always wanted to know about entrepreneurship. By presenting an easy-to-follow methodology for building successful companies, the authors help aspiring entrepreneurs focus their efforts in the right direction – without having to learn lessons the hard way. Most importantly, the book is easy, fun and entertaining to read."

Burghardt Tenderich
Professor, Annenberg School for Communication
University of Southern California

JON BURGSTONE AND BILL MURPHY JR.

BREAKTHROUGH

ENTREPRENEURSHIP

THE PROVEN FRAMEWORK

for

BUILDING BRILLIANT NEW BUSINESSES

Farallon Publishing

San Francisco, California
www.farallonpublishing.com

Library of Congress Control Number: 2011937440

ISBN-13: 978-0983961109

To Ben and Nate,

and the adventures ahead…

and

to J.F. Murphy

CONTENTS

MODULE 1

"Destruction, however painful, is the necessary price of creative progress toward a better material life. But the correct sequence is vital: creative innovation first, then the destruction of obstacles that lie in its way."

- Joseph Schumpeter

THE DRIVING FORCES IN ENTREPRENEURSHIP

You deeply want to become an extraordinary entrepreneur, but you don't know where to begin. You don't have enough money; or else you've got money, but you wouldn't feel right risking it. You're too young; or else you're too old, and the chance has already passed you by. You can't seem to come up with the right idea; or else, you're overwhelmed with ideas and you can't seem to settle on one.

Even the most successful entrepreneurs have moments of self-doubt. It's only human. The next time you stop believing in yourself, though, think of Robin Chase.

With her 40th birthday in the rearview mirror, Chase had been out of the workforce for a year taking care of her three young children. Despite her strong desire to become an entrepreneur, she'd never been able to develop an idea that didn't eventually reveal a fatal flaw. She wondered if she'd ever find the right business.

Then, the big entrepreneurial idea she'd been searching for pretty much pulled up and parked in front of her at a Cambridge, Massachusetts cafe.

A friend of Chase's named Antje Danielson had just returned from a trip to her native Germany, and when they met for coffee, Danielson was eager to talk. Things were changing so fast overseas. She'd seen a bold new business in Berlin: a rental car company that offered cars by the hour instead of the day or the week.

Why hadn't anybody done that here? Danielson wondered.

Yeah, Chase thought. *Why indeed?*

Neither Chase nor Danielson had worked in the automobile industry. Chase didn't even like to drive. Yet Zipcar, the company the two women cofounded out of Chase's home, is now the world leader, with a half million customers, 8,000 vehicles, and almost 500 employees. It all but created the car-sharing industry in America.

In the process of building Zipcar, Chase became a respected voice on transportation policy and the environment. She impacts things that matter to her from a platform she could hardly have imagined a decade ago. She's talked at the global Technology, Entertainment and Design conference (better known as TED) and she speaks to standing-room crowds at top universities. *Time* magazine called her one of the 100 most influential people in America. When we caught up with her recently, she was launching another new company and marveling that she'd convinced an influential think tank to reevaluate its entire position on a transportation policy for the United States government.

"I just got this report and recommendation," she told us, "and they even say---*this is 180 degrees from what we were going to do.* Billions and billions of dollars, and I just changed how it's going to be done. I think that's way cool."

It is way cool. But how does it happen? How does a middle-class, 40-something mother of three move from the coffee shop to the corner office?

And here's an even better question: How can you make a similar transition? How can you join the ranks of the extraordinary entrepreneurs?

THE KEYS TO ZIPCAR'S SUCCESS—AND YOURS

There are two key things you need to do to become an extraordinary entrepreneur:

First, learn and embrace the step-by-step practical framework that unfolds on the following pages. We'll show you how to brainstorm a winning business idea, test the heck out of it before you've committed too much time and money, and grow it into something great. The framework itself is reverse-engineered from the successful experiences of hundreds of entrepreneurs we've interviewed and studied over the years.

Second, embrace the attitude of entrepreneurial inevitability. Understand and accept that if you can implement the practical strategies you'll find in *Breakthrough Entrepreneurship,* your odds of success will be much better. History shows that our free market system depends on the work of outsiders like you who spur real progress by overcoming seemingly insurmountable odds. To help make this attitude become second nature, we'll examine the economic forces that make entrepreneurship work, and we'll do that with the help of an early 20th century economist who gave these forces a name: *creative destruction.*

Keep in mind, both keys are essential. You've got to learn <u>how</u> to do it, and you've got to believe you can do it. No practical framework? That's like a football coach who spends all his time on motivational speeches, but never runs practices or teaches his team any plays. No attitude of inevitability? That's like an actor who memorizes a script, but never thinks about the character's motivation, meets the director, or learns about her vision until opening night.

In this module, we'll take the second key first---attitude and creative destruction---and we'll then use the example of Robin Chase and Zipcar to illustrate a quick case study of the entire practical framework. Then, we'll devote the rest of the book to breaking down the process in much greater detail, using examples from many successful new companies and entrepreneurs to demonstrate how you can put it into practice.

TALES OF A SWASHBUCKLING ECONOMIST

Not to malign an entire profession, but most economists can be kind of boring in person. Meet an exception to the rule: Joseph Schumpeter, an Austrian-born professor from the first half of the 20th century who came across as a sort of economic Indiana Jones, only with charts and graphs. There's a story they tell about the university librarian who in 1909 refused to let Schumpeter's students remove books from the building. Schumpeter challenged the man to a duel by swords, sliced him in the shoulder, won the day, and got the books. He was a ladies' man with an outsized ego, fond of telling people that he aspired to become the world's greatest economist, horseman, and lover---and then adding dryly that things weren't going so well with the horses.

Schumpeter had nearly become destitute as a child after his father died in the 1890s. His mother reinvented their family, however, by packing up for Vienna and basically assuming airs of nobility. Her son grew up to become an academic, rose quickly through the professorial ranks, served as Austria's finance minister in the early 1920s---but then lost everything in the stock market. Schumpeter landed on his feet at a university in neighboring Germany and then fled the country after the Nazis rose to power. Penniless once more in the United States in 1932, he finally found a home at Harvard University, where he spent his last two decades.

Schumpeter was prolific---the author of dozens of books and articles in both German and English---but the work he's most famous for is 1942's *Capitalism, Socialism, and Democracy.* He theorized within its pages that progress in a free society inevitably depends on big, messy disruptions. He studied how great innovations almost always cause short-term pain and insecurity even while they improve peoples' lives in the long run. The short-term economic pain could even be a positive force because it created still more opportunity.

The automobile disrupted the horse and buggy, for example. The factory wiped out the blacksmith shop. Painful as these developments were for livery stable owners and blacksmiths, they represented great progress for just about everyone else. They probably even spurred some of those displaced workers to create promising innovations that they wouldn't have considered otherwise.

For all his skillful swordplay and theories, Schumpeter was only a modest success as an academic in his lifetime. Overshadowed by other economists, he also suffered from a note of awkward timing in his work. The world had just emerged from the Great Depression when he wrote *Capitalism, Socialism, and Democracy.* It might be hard to dream up a less appealing argument for that shell-shocked time than the idea that disruption and lack of economic security were necessary, inevitable, and even positive things.

Schumpeter died in 1950, at the dawn of the information age, a time of accelerating technological progress that makes *creative destruction* much more clear and understandable. Think about how much faster things move now than they did just a few years ago---the books we read, the methods we use to communicate with each other, the ways in which we entertain ourselves. The entities behind most of the goods and services we use are constantly being reshaped and even replaced by newcomers and outsiders. Then, those upstarts grow, mature, and even dominate---only to be eventually killed off themselves. The whole process happens over and over, at an impressive pace.

What's more, as we dig down into the history of these influencers of *creative destruction*, we'll find that there's almost always a single person, or at most a small group of people, who are responsible for the upheaval. In other words, David defeating Goliath isn't the exception; it's often the rule. It turns out there is always a Gandhi standing up to the British Empire, or a Toyota entering the U.S. market and beating the Big Three automakers. At any given time, there's almost always a 19-year-old in a dorm room somewhere, trying to build a company that will change the world.

Maybe you've heard of the Peter Principle, the idea that in any bureaucracy, each employee will eventually rise to the level of his own incompetence. Well, park it behind what we might call the Schumpeter Principle: *Wherever there's an entrenched economic behemoth, there's an extraordinary outsider taking aim---with genuinely good chances of winning.*

So, what does all of this have to do with Robin Chase, or with Zipcar, or thousands of other extraordinary entrepreneurs out there? What does it have to do with you?

Simple. Once you have absorbed and mastered the tools you'll find on the pages that follow, recognize that economic forces are on your side. There's a wind at your back. Your entrepreneurial efforts- --if they're designed well and tested according to the framework we'll be discussing---can work because they're *supposed* to work. That is how the world has progressed for centuries. If anything, the pace of change is only accelerating. Hop on, strap in, and enjoy the ride.

HOW TO WORK HARD IN THE RIGHT DIRECTION

"This is the elevator pitch that I have given probably close to a thousand times," Robin Chase replied when asked to describe Zipcar's business.

Zipcar parks cars throughout dense metropolitan areas and university towns. You make a reservation online or by telephone for a very specific car in a specific location and that reservation is sent wirelessly to the car. You hold your membership card on a spot in the windshield and that unlocks the door, enables the ignition and opens the billing record. People drive round trip and park back in that same reserved parking space. The billing record is closed and you are all done.

That sounds pretty sensible now that it exists. But what steps did Chase take to go from a casual conversation about an interesting idea to building a real company? She had a few mentors and peers that she could turn to, which certainly helped---a classmate who had started a company, for example, and a professional investor she'd met at a social function. Beyond that, she was starting from scratch. How did she make it happen?

It worked because Chase was methodical, because she followed the good structural advice of people who'd succeeded before her, and because she intuitively understood the forces of creative destruction. We've found after researching hundreds of these stories that the practical steps logically self-organize into seven components.

They include:

1. Find and fill an important unmet customer need.

2. Plan for profitability.

3. Strive for sustainability.

4. Establish credibility.

5. Gather necessary resources.

6. Lead and manage effectively.

7. Maintain balance and learn to enjoy the ride.

FIND AND FILL AN IMPORTANT UNMET CUSTOMER NEED

If you find yourself lost at any point as you're planning, launching, or running a venture, the solution is always to let the customer be your compass. From the very start with Zipcar, Chase focused on figuring out who her customers were and how her idea for a company could help satisfy their needs---even needs they didn't recognize they had.

"There really was a light bulb that went on in my head when my partner said, what do you think of this idea?" Robin Chase told us. "I personally, as a user, would want to do it."

That last sentence is important. Chase recognized that she was probably her own ideal customer---an urban, cost-conscious consumer who didn't like the hassles of car ownership but who wanted the freedom to travel by automobile when she needed to. That gave her an instinctive sense of what similar customers' real needs might be. She talked about providing customers an easier way to access a car and also giving them freedom---things she craved herself.

Moreover, we can easily identify at least three strategies that Robin used in coming up with the idea for Zipcar that we also find over and over in other extraordinary entrepreneur case studies. For example, you might observe that Chase:

- Adapted a successful idea from another market to one she understood: in this case, from Germany to the United States.

- Cross-pollinated between two or more ideas: car sharing, the Internet and mobile technology, which turned out to be integral to the company's development.

- Identified a niche market that wasn't being served: city-dwellers who wanted to save money, cared about the environment, only needed to drive sporadically because they had access to public transportation, or didn't particularly like driving or owning cars.

Customer needs don't have to be overt or practical. Maybe some customers want to *seem* environmentally conscious, just as intently as they want to *be* environmentally conscious. Chase's company might offer the experience of being a Zipcar member as much as the practical benefits of joining.

Bottom line, Chase didn't need to dream up the entire concept of a car-sharing service. She could look at what was working in Europe, consider how the American market might be similar or different and think as well about how recently developed technology could improve the business over what was being done elsewhere.

PLAN FOR PROFITABILITY

The profit motive drives the economic world. Whether you use your profits to surround yourself with luxury or to help the less fortunate, earning more money is generally a desirable goal. Moreover, there's not a lot of good in coming up with a great solution to your customers' needs if you can't stay in business to serve them. If Chase had one advantage, it's that coupled with her desire to do good in the world she harbored a strong predisposition toward seeking profits.

In fact, Chase had spent several months before her fateful conversation with Antje Danielson working on another startup idea that hadn't panned out precisely because she couldn't figure out how to make it profitable. Her earlier idea had been to build an Internet market through which Third World artists and craftspeople could sell artwork directly to First World customers. As with Zipcar, Chase recognized that she would be her own prototypical customer and her research showed millions of others out there just like her. However, the costs of transferring money and goods were just too high at the time. (Later, a company called Etsy figured out how to overcome this problem. It now facilitates about $400 million of these kinds of transactions each year.)

Chase similarly planned to spend months doing the math on Zipcar before she launched, studying and adapting the European model. As an example, she learned that the European companies were small and that they charged their members large upfront fees---the equivalent of hundreds of dollars---to join. Why? Because they needed the cash to buy or lease their cars. Robin thought about whether that was likely to work in an American consumer culture. Ultimately, she decided she had to find a way to make the initial membership fees much lower.

She learned that overseas, with almost no marketing effort, car-sharing companies were growing at 30 percent or more a year. But the North American market was both large and untouched. There were only a few small competitors in the market---one in Oregon, a second in Seattle and a third in Quebec.

Moreover, Boston and neighboring Cambridge provided an ideal test market. The metropolitan area had a dense population and it was home to some of the most expensive parking and insurance rates in the country. There were many people moving in and out all the time, and many of them were sensitive to cost concerns. Chase realized she could try it in Boston with just a handful of cars, see if things took hold, and expand if they worked out. It offered a chance to obtain *maximum information for minimum cost.*

With the first draft of the business plan completed, Chase tried to refine how many people might use Zipcar, how often they would rent, what buying or leasing each car would cost the company, and what the overhead would be---and thus how much they had to charge in order to break even. She realized as well that this would probably require several iterations. In fact, just a few months after the company launched, when she analyzed the hard data she'd accumulated, Chase saw that some of her calculations had been wrong. Zipcar wasn't charging enough to break even, and so she was left with little choice but to announce her mistake to her members and raise the daily rates. These sorts of business model iterations are common and natural. Embrace them as learning opportunities.

STRIVE FOR SUSTAINABILITY

Sustainable ventures have competitive advantages over others that might enter the market and they follow business models that work well in the long run. One way to build these kinds of advantages is to strive to play a different game from your competitors. For example, Chase didn't pursue the same customers that the established, billion-dollar rental car companies targeted, such as business travelers who would rent cars at airports and hotels. Instead, she targeted a niche market of city dwellers---often somewhat liberal or even hipster in outlook. She wasn't just renting cars. She was renting an image. Many members felt like they were part of a movement as much or more than they felt like mere customers.

"I wanted to make people feel that if they had to choose between Zipcar and Hertz, or Zipcar and Enterprise," she later recalled, "that they would choose Zipcar because we were their personal local community service, and not a more pasteurized big corporate company."

Similarly, Zipcar offered ease of use. Nobody else out there was doing this kind of thing in Boston at the time, or else in the other markets they slowly expanded to. Theoretically, one could rent a car from Hertz or Avis at the airport for a short trip, but this was impractical for the average Zipcar target customer.

From the beginning, Chase recognized that wireless technology and the Internet would give Zipcar a significant advantage over anything that had come before. She wanted members to be able to go online to rent a car and then she wanted her company's computers to be able to unlock the doors remotely. The system also had to be able to transmit how long the users drove the car so that Zipcar could charge them the right rental fee.

Additionally, Chase found a marketing advantage in that, statistically, European car sharing companies removed more than seven cars from the road for each one they added to their fleet because members decided they didn't need to own their private vehicles anymore. That meant she could market the company not just as convenient and economical, but also as the environmentally friendly alternative to car ownership.

Chase spent several months thinking about the business model and there were some advantages to the ideas she developed. For example, requiring a significant but reasonable upfront fee to join made it less likely that members would ditch Zipcar for any new competitor; they'd already have a sunk cost with Chase's company. She locked up key partners, as well---forging relationships with the municipal governments in and around Boston, as well as the MBTA, which runs Boston-area subways and busses. Moreover, she braced herself for the inevitable day when Hertz, Avis, and the other big rental car companies would enter the market, and she tried to create metaphorical land mines that would make it more painful for them to do so. Everything about her model was designed to force bigger companies to cannibalize their core businesses if they wanted to compete with her.

"They had to come in kicking and screaming, because Zipcar really is disruptive," she said in an interview, in that it destroyed the minimum 24-hour rental period the traditional companies counted on. "From a business perspective they had to break something that was quite favorable to them."

ESTABLISH CREDIBILITY

They say in the military that no battle plan survives contact with the enemy. Smart entrepreneurs know that every business must react and adjust its plan once it makes contact with the market. Even though Chase believed she had done a thorough job of researching the potential for a car-sharing company and putting together a savvy business plan, she had to convince potential investors, employees, customers, and other stakeholders that *she* was the one to put that plan into action.

You might imagine that this is something an entrepreneur does over time. In recent years, as Chase has looked back at her success, she says one of the keys was to pick manageably sized pieces of the project, complete them, and then build on her success. This wasn't so much a strategy as it was a compulsion. She felt like her credibility was on the line with each step.

"It felt, as I say, inexorable," she told us. "After this momentum that we'd built, I felt like there was no turning back. Internally, in my mind, I felt a huge pressure to open up and get going and put cars on the road and have people using them. It was totally self-imposed, but in my mind they were external factors."

Of course, she later realized that some of her self-imposed deadlines were a bit arbitrary. ("To the city of Cambridge," she asked rhetorically, "would it have mattered if I had opened two months later?") Still, by forcing herself to adhere to her schedule and follow through on the things she'd said she was going to do, she built credibility.

It paid off. When Zipcar launched with a lime green Volkswagen New Beetle, a white Golf and a white Passat parked in Cambridge, Chase had already built momentum that led to press coverage, more members and a loyal following. An Associated Press reporter noticed the first Zipcar Beetle on the street, contacted the company and wrote a national story. Weeks later, Chase was featured on NPR's *Morning Edition*, and in several stories in *The Boston Globe*. The coolness of the concept caught on and the headlines were uniformly positive, with a sort of *"Welcome to the future... why didn't we think of this?"* vibe.

There was more to building credibility than simply getting press coverage, though. Some of Chase's early mentors advised her that when it came time to raise money she focus on getting the most sophisticated investors possible. She dug through her contacts and her memory, finding any excuse or introduction she could to pitch to smart investors. Even if they didn't wind up investing, the fact that well-known venture capitalists took meetings with her and took her seriously built credibility with others she hoped would become stakeholders.

GATHER RESOURCES

What resources do you need to start a rental car company? It turns out that you need variations of the same things you need to start virtually every other kind of venture: *time, people,* and *money.*

Chase dedicated her own time to start with. She devoted basically 100 percent to investigating the venture even before she decided for sure to start it. Her cofounder, Antje, kept her day job but devoted time as well. Chase's husband wound up working on it too.

They needed others too, and with money short in the beginning there was a lot of emphasis on getting people to work for the promise of a better future, instead of more traditional compensation (i.e., money). Perhaps their biggest early personnel expenditure had to do with the fact that they needed a talented programmer who could build the wireless network they would need.

While Chase wanted to keep expenses as low as possible at first, she did need some money. She raised her first $50,000 from a single angel investor---a business school classmate who had enjoyed success as an entrepreneur and who believed in the Zipcar idea and wanted to help. It's a classic story, though: continually raising money can be a huge distraction for entrepreneurs. Chase put together another $325,000 from a series of investors, and kept trying to raise a venture capital round in the several million-dollar range. Doing so proved very difficult. At one point, Zipcar was down to its last $68. While Chase was ultimately successful, it's hard to overstate the toll it took on her personally.

"I was a complete shell of a human after going through those four or five months," she explained, including the thousands of hours of work, and the continual up-and-down experience of thinking she'd nearly closed on the funds, having deals fall apart, and trying to put them back together again.

Wise entrepreneurs scrounge for inexpensive resources, in order to avoid the need to raise capital. As an example, Chase needed parking spaces for each Zipcar. One economical solution was to recruit the city of Cambridge as a partner, and convince the city to lease her municipal parking spaces for just $1 a month for the first year. She needed marketing and advertising, and so Zipcar turned its cars and the signs reserving their parking spaces into mini-billboards. Chase put a lot of effort into getting the cars' look and the company logo just right. They plastered the logo on the passenger door and trunk, but also decided to keep the driver's side door clear so that the "Zipster" behind the wheel wouldn't be constantly reminded that the car was doubling as an advertisement.

LEAD AND MANAGE EFFECTIVELY

Leading people and managing resources effectively is a familiar struggle for many entrepreneurs. "While the idea and the conception and all that really did come together quickly," Chase told us, "my understanding at the start of what that meant in terms of execution was infantile. I had no idea what that really meant. You start, and you go day by day, and it gets more and more complex on a slow path of increasingly complexity. And then, there's a certain point when you realize, I'm thinking about and doing this day and night."

In our discussions, and in Chase's public appearances, she generally has a peaceful, reasoned demeanor. She doesn't seem the type to go off on a tirade. You can imagine her in one of those old airplane disaster movies, explaining calmly over the radio to a passenger on a stricken jumbo jet how to land the plane. Especially in the early days at Zipcar, however, she had to learn to be assertive with her employees and colleagues, confident that she was the one who had come up with the idea, who had researched every facet of the market and who had taken the first risks in starting out. Zipcar had a limited window of opportunity and limited resources, but Chase also had the benefit of months of research and a unique insight into how to make the company work. She tried to force her vision, and she didn't share the daily troubles with employees who couldn't impact them.

"I went through lots of drama, and went and raised $4 million over three or four months, and it took every pound of flesh that I had," she explained. But, she added, "I didn't share any of the calamities with any of my staff, just the one or two at the top."

Chase created urgency among her people, driving them to adhere to deadlines and get the company moving quickly. She formed a powerful coalition by bringing in investors, local governments, and the members themselves. She appealed to their desire to achieve something huge---"change the way people own cars." And she made sure that everyone in the organization could speak with one voice when they described what they were trying to do to the outside world. She removed obstacles and created short-term wins---and celebrated them. Then, as they achieved their milestones, Chase cajoled her team to attack the next objectives: more members, more cities, better technology, and greater impact.

MAINTAIN BALANCE AND LEARN TO ENJOY THE RIDE

Starting a company is exciting, admirable, and worthy--- and it's also really hard work. It can often take a severe toll on the entrepreneur. Chase had three young children---ages 6, 9, and 12---when she launched Zipcar, and she's frank now about the fact that it was all but impossible to build a company and take care of her family at the same time. Something had to give, and for a while, she acknowledges, that something was her family.

"That first summer, I was working day and night," she recalled. "My daughter said, 'Do you ever sleep?' At 8 p.m. when she went to bed, I'd be at the computer. At 6 a.m. or 7 a.m. she'd wake up and I was still there."

You'll see the metaphor many times in this book: *entrepreneurship is a roller coaster.* One week you're being interviewed on national television about your innovative idea; the next week you're close to missing payroll. Then you close a big deal; then you lose a key employee; then you make a great product improvement; then you screw up a financial projection. Ups and downs, highs and lows, over and over.

So here's an important question: How did Robin Chase stay sane? For one thing, she and her husband eventually worked out how to balance their work and family lives a bit better, but there were several other factors. First, Zipcar was thoroughly infused with Chase's personal values. She cared deeply about the environment and human sustainability and she felt that every day she went to work at Zipcar she was both building a company and addressing global issues.

She said she started Zipcar "with 100 percent certainty that I was in this to grow, and it would be a great company, but I would not have been willing to devote 100 hours a week to something with no social upside."

Second, Chase embraced entrepreneurship itself. It seems like this should be self-evident, but we're not sure that it is: If you want to become an extraordinary entrepreneur, it helps a lot if you're driven to create things, and if you actually take pleasure in the process of entrepreneurship. Chase clearly learned to enjoy this ride. She eventually transitioned out of the management of Zipcar, and she has gone on to start a consulting firm and another Internet startup. When we talked with her recently, she was in Paris working on yet another new company: a peer-to-peer car-sharing service, through which members could rent their own cars to one another.

(Wait a minute. Paris? France has a large population of adults who don't own cars, Chase explained, and added that the success of bike-sharing and other innovative transportation models suggests the French might catch on more quickly. She hopes to build the company and bring the model back to America, much as she did with Zipcar.)

Third, Chase says she wasn't in it for the money. In fact, she jokes with her daughter that the main thing she wanted to do with her post-Zipcar windfall was to buy more gourmet olives each time she went to the grocery store.

"I have to make a living," she told us, "but my requirements on making a living don't include aspirations of having a Jaguar and six houses. I was in Louis Vuitton the other day, and I'm uninterested in $4,000 handbags."

By the way, don't take this to mean you shouldn't want to become financially independent. That has its upside, believe us. But it's not everything, and it's not necessarily a key to happiness.

Finally, for Chase, there is the sense of impact. When she gives a talk at TED, or turns on her computer to find emails from policymakers asking her opinions on transportation and the environment, those experiences become their own reward. It's the chance to impact things that she cares about deeply.

"I really like efficiency and beautifully designed things," she told us. "All those peoples' cars parked uselessly, and my tax dollars at work. Who doesn't want to see it spent more beautifully? A lot of my thought work now is around excess capacity and tapping into excess capacity. When you make an efficient use of something, it's beautiful."

THE BIG PICTURE

Robin Chase's entrepreneurial journey wasn't perfect, of course. There are things she'd probably do differently if she were to start again from square one. Moreover, you don't have to be the kind of person who loves Zipcar to benefit from her story. We've presented it here as an introductory case, a sort of overview of the concepts we'll describe in greater detail in the modules that follow.

Chase was smart, educated, and ambitious, but---and we don't think she'll mind us saying this---she was otherwise an ordinary person. Had you been there at the cafe in Cambridge that September day, you would have been hard pressed to pick out which customer was about to create a dynamic new company and change an entire industry.

And yet, she made the transformation. That's inspiring, and it's instructive. Whether you hope to launch the next great billion-dollar tech company, or simply start a small business in your hometown, the principles behind Chase's story apply. From finding and filling important customer needs, to learning to enjoy the entrepreneurial ride, there's a common framework on the following pages, and it works.

Remember: *creative destruction.* Zipcar disrupts other industries (the traditional rental car industry, the automobile industry itself, even the public transportation network). But it was inevitable that eventually someone would do so, and it was highly probable that the *someone* would be an outsider.

So, how does an aspiring extraordinary entrepreneur get started? Where's your cup of coffee in the Cambridge cafe? It's all great and good if you have a flash of brilliance and recognize an opportunity in front of you. But what if that just doesn't happen?

Those are the questions we'll ask and answer in the next module: Where do good entrepreneurial ideas come from, and how do you find them if you don't know where to look?

MODULE 2

"I find out what the world needs, then I proceed to invent."

- Thomas Edison

IDEAS PART 1: IDEA GENERATION AND EVALUATION

You walk into a store and a fantastic new product stops you short. *Why didn't I think of that?* You read about an entrepreneur who made millions solving problems you and your friends have discussed many times. *Why didn't we launch that business?* Or else, the opposite happens. You read about a hot-selling product or service---and you simply can't fathom why it's doing so well.

Where do the best entrepreneurial ideas come from? How can you train yourself to identify the really good ones early? More than that, how do you find ideas that take advantage of your unique ambitions, experience, and talents?

These are questions every entrepreneur faces, and Jim Koch was no exception. He's the founder and CEO of Boston Beer Company, which is now a $400-million-a-year public venture. If you've ever seen Koch in the television commercials for Samuel Adams Boston Lager you'd be forgiven for thinking that he was born knowing he was here on Earth to brew beer. But the truth is that when Koch first decided he wanted to be an entrepreneur he had no idea even what industry he wanted to pursue.

To understand how Koch found his entrepreneurial destiny, we have to go back to the 1980s. He was in his 30s then, working at a lucrative, prestigious job at a top business strategy consulting firm. Years of near-constant business travel had worn on him. Koch decided to try his hand at entrepreneurship as an alternative to the much more common path for business consultants at the time, joining the management of one of the firm's Fortune 500 clients.

Facing a true blank slate, Koch approached matters as he'd been trained. He made a list of the hottest industries---those with the most investor interest and the highest growth rates---and analyzed the opportunities to be found in each.

Personal computers were new and popular at the time, so that seemed a natural place to look. The problem was that Koch barely used them, and so he would have little expertise to draw on. He next thought about the up-and-coming video game industry. He had friends who had started companies in that industry and who had made a lot of money, but Koch acknowledged that he barely knew his *Donkey Kong* from his *Missile Command*.

He analyzed opportunities in the booming healthcare and telecommunications industries, but each time, he walked away with the same reaction: *That's not me. I don't know how to do that.*

Instead of chasing after other peoples' opportunities, Koch changed his approach. He thought about where he might have specific knowledge or experience that would give him advantages and make his entrepreneurial adventures more personal and fun. He took stock of who he was, what he knew, and what interested him. He was a father and a husband. He loved the outdoors---hiking, camping, and climbing---and he had been an Outward Bound mountaineering instructor. He was a consultant who had analyzed business opportunities for some of the most successful companies in America.

Last but not least, he really liked beer.

Now, don't get the wrong idea. American bars are *full* of people who really like beer, but the difference was that Koch thought of himself as a beer drinker with a refined palate. To his mind, the American beer industry had never really recovered after Prohibition. American beer was limited to a few varieties of light-tasting beers brewed by a small handful of big companies. Foreign breweries shipped their more varied products to U.S. shores, but the product was often stale or skunked by the time it arrived. American beer drinkers couldn't get a glass of full, fresh-tasting beer.

Moreover, Koch came from a brewing family. He could count back six generations in his ancestry, and find brewers all along the way back to Germany. His father had retired from a brewery--- albeit reluctantly, in the face of competition from some of those big

American companies---and so he was familiar both with brewing beer and with how the industry worked.

"I kept coming back to brewing," Koch told us. "It was in my family, so I knew a lot about it. I'd been drinking beer, but knowledgably and mindfully, and ... that led me to the simple insight on which Sam Adams was built. This was in 1984, and I said, you can't get great beer in the United States today, but I know how to brew great beer and get it to people fresh. I can do that. I can put the best glass of beer in America in front of a beer drinker. I can make the best beer in America."

As a beer industry veteran, Koch's father was highly skeptical at first, and there were some slow, discouraging days in the beginning. It took years, long hours, hard work, savvy strategic choices, and a little bit of serendipity. Eventually, however, Koch's early insights into the tastes of a certain type of customer, and the way he might fill those customers' needs, proved right. Boston Beer Company is now the largest American-owned brewery (Anheuser-Busch, Miller, and Coors have all either merged or were acquired by foreign companies).

So, was it really that simple? Well, yes and no. It's vital to come up with an excellent idea, of course. However, it's another thing entirely to be able to build a solid business plan around that idea, and execute. So, what made Koch so confident right up front that he'd be able to brew beer at scale, and convince other people to try it? How did he figure out how to take on the big breweries?

And most importantly, how can _you_ apply his strategies to find the big ideas that can help you become an extraordinary entrepreneur?

AN INSIGHTFUL APPROACH TO RISK

Most of this module is about brainstorming, but first we're going to briefly examine the concept of risk in entrepreneurship. Doing so will help train you to separate good ideas from marginal ones quickly and efficiently. We'll spend some time on this---perhaps more time than you think at the outset is warranted---but there's a crucial reason: _If you don't absorb and implement the concepts we'll be talking about in this module and the two that follow, then nothing else you learn here will matter._

It's often suggested that entrepreneurs simply have higher risk tolerance than other people, or else that they're blind to risks that "more sensible" people might heed. We think that a better way to look at it is that entrepreneurs are like comedians. They see the same world the rest of us do, but they perceive the patterns differently. Much as a comedian might think about life's routine rhythms and laugh at the absurdities, an extraordinary entrepreneur learns to look at life's frustrations and recognize the opportunities to innovate.

As an entrepreneur, your goals include garnering advantages that make your venture as much of a sure thing as possible. That means methodically assessing it against the two inherent categories of risk in any entrepreneurial venture: **business risk** and **technical risk**.

Business risk refers to questions like whether or not there is truly a market for the product or service. What is the competition like? How much profit can we make on each unit we produce? *Technical risk* refers to questions related to whether you can produce the product efficiently, consistently, and effectively.

Much more to come on this, but for now, just keep the concepts in the back of your mind as you brainstorm. Most entrepreneurs find that they more naturally address one or the other type of risk, but addressing both business risk and technical risk is vital.

BRAINSTORMING NEW IDEAS

Good news: Entrepreneurs rarely need to come up with an original idea completely out of the blue. In fact, jumping too far ahead can create problems for an entrepreneur, because innovations face short and lonely lives if they're too advanced. (Customers often don't adapt and use them.) Often, especially for first-time entrepreneurs, it can be better to look for more incremental steps forward or else to try to cross-pollinate two (or more) accepted ideas or insights: Take Insight A, add Insight B, and see if they lead you toward a great new venture idea.

Here's the real trick. Ideally, the ideas or insights that you cross-pollinate will contain within them the seeds of how to reduce either business or technical risks. In fact, one early test of your business ideas can be to ask if the insights you come up with lead you immediately to think of ways to reduce risk compared to less-innovative competitors.

Think about how this worked for the two entrepreneurs whose stories we've looked at in depth so far. The original idea behind Zipcar, for example, was basically the fusion of two insights. Robin Chase intuitively sensed (and, more importantly, later researched and proved) that there were many people in urban areas who would want to use cars without actually owning them---an insight about the size of her potential market that leads directly to an assessment of the business risk in her idea. Then, she cross-pollinated that insight with a nascent understanding of how wireless technology could enable a company to spread its cars around a city, thus addressing her technical risk.

Similarly, Jim Koch's original idea to brew and sell beer emerged from two insights: First, he had a 150-year-old family recipe for beer stored away in the attic. Between his amateur beer-making experience and his father's industry knowledge, he had a good sense of how to brew barrels by the thousands, insights that reduced his technical risk. Meanwhile, he combined that with his understanding that many potential customers shared similar palates, as well as his experience advising top companies on management and operations---insights into market size, leadership, and management, which reduced his business risk.

In retrospect, Koch's insights and his risk assessments seem spot-on, but of course he couldn't have known that for sure at first.

The story of the early days of Boston Beer Company is also instructive because it is about getting *maximum information for minimum cost.* Koch tested his theories, kept expenses low, and kept his overall exposure to a minimum.

"I needed to do two things really, really well," he told us: "brew great beer and work my butt off to sell it. I really focused on those and in some ways ignored other stuff."

For example, Koch contracted with an older, established brewery to use his recipe to produce the first kegs of Samuel Adams Boston Lager rather than establish his own facility. He built credibility by winning brewing contests, rather than pursuing an expensive marketing campaign. He didn't even have an office at first. Working with his ex-secretary who became his partner, he went bar-to-bar in Boston, trying to convince owners and bartenders to try his product.

"I literally did not have a desk for years," he recalled. "I couldn't make beer in an office. I couldn't sell beer in an office, so I didn't need a desk. If I had to go sit somewhere it would be in a bar. It would be with the customers."

Besides saving money, it meant he was there in person to listen to what beer owners and beer drinkers wanted. He could adjust his product and sales pitch to meet their preferences. It's hard to find a better way to launch a business than one that lets you do so cheaply while simultaneously getting instant feedback from your customers.

Developing Possible Business Ideas

So, how do you make this kind of risk-reducing, idea-generating, *A-meets-B* strategy work for you? How do you go from blank slate to brilliant idea? Start by taking stock of what you do, what you know, and who you are. If you were to simply describe yourself to a new friend, what cultural, professional or personal experiences would come up first? Maybe write a two-page autobiography to get you started. What points would you absolutely have to include?

Is there an industry you're familiar with or a group of underserved customers with whom you identify? Be expansive. Regardless of your age or background, you likely have the spark of a big idea. What do you and your friends want or need? Look at changes in technology and other contextual shifts. Think about what's different in the world today from five years ago. What opportunities have arisen as a result? Even things you might otherwise think of as weaknesses can often be turned into strengths, because they might help you understand what a target customer will want or need.

So, if you're a 30-year-old business consultant or banker who would love to start a company but who doesn't have much operational experience, take heart. The exposure you've had to many different industries and business processes might serve you very well, especially if you can figure out how to combine two or more of them together. If you're a 23-year-old software engineer who would like to be working for yourself instead of making other people rich, think of what you understand about your peers that others wouldn't know.

Maybe you're a 55-year-old former assembly line worker. You might feel down on your luck, but the truth is that you have insights into what people like you need and dream of that the uninitiated could never comprehend.

Even if you're a teenaged high school student, you know much more about your peers than people even a decade older than you do. In this period of intense, repeated, creative destruction, younger people sometimes have an advantage because the state of the art is the only thing they've known. You don't have to unlearn 20 or 30 years of inapplicable misconceptions. That's an asset, and it might be part of what you marry with another asset to find a great idea.

For inspiration, look at first-time entrepreneurs like Michael Dell, who started PCs Limited (now known as Dell Inc.) in his University of Texas dorm room at age 18. Mark Zuckerberg started Facebook at 19. Bill Gates was 21 when he left Harvard to co-found Microsoft. Yahoo!, Google, Oracle, Apple, and many other companies were founded by very young people.

On the other end, don't be concerned if you've reached a later stage in life. Harlan Sanders was 62 before he opened the first Kentucky Fried Chicken. Sam Walton was 44 when he started the first true Wal-Mart in 1962. Don Fisher was 41 when he and his wife Doris founded The Gap, which later expanded to include Old

Navy and Banana Republic. He left a $3 billion estate when he died including one of the world's most important collections of post-World War II art.

The human eye is built to notice physical movement, and the extraordinary entrepreneur similarly picks up quickly on cultural movements. So, concentrate on what has changed in your own life in the past year---or the past five years, or 10. Have you gotten married? Had kids? Gotten braces for your teeth or changed your appearance? Battled a disease? Shifted careers? What does your personal experience lead you to consider about our common experiences?

Here's an example: Suppose you or your family bought a home in 2001. You could have sold it and tripled your money in 2006, but you held on, watching your equity disappear, until you finally sold in 2011. Think about what your experience tells you about how the entire U.S. housing market has changed in five years. How do your peers now approach the problem of finding a suitable place to live? How do you feel about investing, about politics, about the American Dream? Whenever there is a change in the context, inevitably, there is also an opportunity.

So, who knows better: a 50-year-old engineer in a cubicle at Cisco Systems Inc., or the customers who have grown up using Cisco products? Trick question. The answer is both. Great ideas can come from anyone who truly understands a market and its customers' needs.

SPREADING PROVEN TRENDS ACROSS GEOGRAPHIES

If you don't see an obvious cross-pollination idea, sometimes the solution is to let the world do the cross-pollinating for you. Twenty-five years ago, Americans visiting Europe would often remark on the café culture in major cities. Why was it that Paris, Vienna, Venice, and Prague had vibrant coffee shops on virtually every street, but not the U.S.? Didn't Americans want places to gather, linger, read, and talk? Of course, a few enterprising entrepreneurs did notice and they combined European cafes with an understanding of American consumers. Now it seems there is a Starbucks on every corner in every city in America.

Explore what trends are hot in other cultures, and see if they can be transported to where you live. As an example, the Japanese market is famous for being full of early technology adapters. So if you want to figure out what tech products are likely to be hot in the United States in six months to two years, you might take a trip to Tokyo, ride the subway, walk through the malls of Shibuya, and figure out what new devices the affluent youth there are using.

You don't have to go that far, though. Ask yourself, what are the hipsters doing in Brooklyn? What are the sports fans doing in Chicago? What are the soccer moms doing in Houston? What are the publicity hounds doing on the red carpets of Los Angeles?

One example of spreading products to new geographies started after expensive gourmet cupcakes grew very popular in New York

City. Smart entrepreneurs around the country copied the notion, pairing the proven business model with their understanding of local markets. The television network TLC even launched a reality show about one of them. Instead of starting with a new product that hadn't been tried and tested---say, a truffle trattoria in Trenton, or a baba ghanoush bakery in Boise---these entrepreneurs spread the New York City cupcake trend that had already proven successful. We see this happen all the time, with all kinds of trends in food, fashion, and culture.

Now, think back to *technical risk* and *business risk*. Taking a proven business model and trying it somewhere new can reduce both elements. If someone can bake gourmet cupcakes in New York City, then from a technical standpoint it's a pretty safe bet you can probably also do so in Naperville, Illinois or Providence, Rhode Island. And from a business risk standpoint, you can literally begin your risk-reduction research by sitting in a New York City bakery for a few hours. Just be sure to hit the gym for an extra hour afterward.

Keep your eye out for business ideas where you can learn fast and get feedback quickly from your customers---much like how Jim Koch virtually set up shop in his customers' bars. Look for opportunities where you can get started inexpensively and where you can scale quickly and profitably if things work out as you hope. The theory of creative destruction tells us that when it comes to entrepreneurship, if you build it, the competition will come. So your best bet at winning is to get yourself established, and capitalize on your head start.

Let's use the cupcake example again. In the first decade of the 21st century, little gourmet cupcakes were featured in a memorable *Saturday Night Live* video short that went viral and the characters on *Sex and the City* ate them on screen, thus exposing the New York trend to a much broader audience. It makes sense that a sort of copycat phenomenon would lead enterprising entrepreneurs to open similar businesses in other U.S. cities. But it also helped immensely that fresh cupcakes are inherently a local product, so entrepreneurs' local knowledge could make for a big advantage. Boxes of cupcakes don't travel well. The founders of a successful bakery in New York City might want to open new stores in Philadelphia and Boston, but they'd need new infrastructure to bake cupcakes in their new stores. Other entrepreneurs who moved quickly enough could open bakeries in their cities and establish beachheads to keep others out of their local cupcake kingdoms.

THINKING INTERNATIONALLY

International cross-pollination goes both ways, and so successful entrepreneurs can often export American business ideas to other countries. Maybe you grew up in the U.S., but your family is from China, or India, or Latin America, and so you understand one of those cultures. Why not combine two things you know about---a successful idea you've seen work in the United States and a foreign culture you've experienced?

For example, Miguel Angel Dávila Guzmán came to the U.S. for his education, but returned to Mexico afterward and launched a chain of American-style movie multiplexes called Cinemex, which he went on to sell for $300 million. Entrepreneur Bo Shao followed a similar path, earning his degrees in the United States but returning to Shanghai, where he started EachNet, China's first successful online auction site, which eBay later bought for about $150 million. An Indian entrepreneur who had studied in the United States returned home to launch IndiaBulls, an online investment mechanism reminiscent of E*TRADE. If you were to go to China or Russia and ask about search engines and social networks, you might hear about things like Baidu and V Kontakte, which are basically localized versions of Google and Facebook.

It hasn't happened yet, but someday we might even find an entrepreneur with an affinity for carb-laden breakfasts and a deep knowledge of foreign cultures. Maybe he or she will figure out how to do a truly international version of the International House of Pancakes.

New Needs and Niches

Another way to ride the coattails of other companies' proven business models is to segment their customers. Figure out which needs and niches they don't fill as well as others and devise solutions.

For example, consider the world of online social networks. As of this writing, it seems likely that Facebook will remain the industry leader at least in the United States. With the possible exception of Google, which had the inestimable advantage of being able to leverage the breadth of services such as Gmail to attract users to Google+, it's unlikely anyone will launch a competing service that will "out-Facebook" Facebook any time soon. That said, there might be niches that Facebook serves less effectively than others, and those niches can mean opportunities.

At its start, Facebook membership was limited to current Harvard University undergraduates and its campus popularity was overwhelming. Mark Zuckerberg and his team did the natural thing, expanding Facebook's reach---first to other Ivy League universities, then to all college students, and finally to anyone with an email address. Now, Facebook has grown so huge that if it were a country, it would be the third largest in the world. Your grandmother is probably on it. The boy or girl you least want to remember from high school has probably tried to "friend" you through it. Well on its way to one billion active users, Facebook can't possibly please everybody all of the time.

So what doors might that open for aspiring entrepreneurs?

LOCALIZATION OR LIMITED ACCESS

Several start-ups have tried to go back to Facebook's roots by limiting access only to members of Ivy League universities, or to students at Big 10 schools, or at small liberal arts colleges. Students at the University of California at Berkeley built a social network with membership limited only to their peers. Alumni from West Point did the same thing. Or what about a company that provides a template to create segmented alumni social networks, and lets the customers figure out how they want to segment themselves?

Of course alma maters and geography aren't the only opportunities. Imagine combining the proven attraction of a limited-access social network with a society or culture you might have some knowledge of---networks for physicians, for example, or writers, or professional engineers. People share lots of personal information on Facebook, and some have grown more and more uncomfortable with the idea over time. Maybe there is room for a social network that gives users more control over privacy settings.

Long-term, of course, the question of whether you could build new competing networks like these *profitably* is a crucial consideration, and one we'll address in the next module.

Entry-Level and Mid-Market Products

Often an innovative company brings a technologically advanced product to market only to experience "*feature-creep.*" If the company thinks its customers want the newest, most advanced features, it can pursue these at all costs. (Clayton Christensen has written extensively about this phenomenon in *The Innovator's Dilemma.*) Left behind, there might be a market for slower adopters who are willing to wait a few years for similar products at a lower price, or who simply don't want all the bells and whistles to begin with. This creates opportunities for other entrepreneurs to come into an established market, and to focus on the lower end.

An obvious example: These days, most automobiles come equipped with standard features that would have seemed luxurious a few decades ago. When is the last time you were in a car that didn't have power windows or air-conditioning? But if you're a consumer looking just for basic transportation on a budget, maybe you don't care as much about having the latest stereo or LED lighting. Maybe you're more interested in driving a new car with a warranty than you are in having rain-sensing, variable intermittent windshield wipers.

Car manufacturers have recognized that there might be an opportunity here, and the result has been vehicles like the Toyota Yaris, Ford Fiesta and Honda Fit. Similarly, modern smart phones include features that would have seemed like science fiction not long ago, but they're fairly expensive. Some niche manufacturers and communications companies have found lots of room for profitability with no-frills phones and low-priced service plans.

BUSINESS EXAMPLE:
MID-MARKET OPPORTUNITIES

Entrepreneur John Osher had worked as a taxi driver, a carpenter, a plumber, a jewelry salesman, a second-hand clothing retailer, an energy conservation innovator and a toy manufacturer. In the late 1990s, this innovator with the roundabout resume was looking for a new challenge. He found it in an unlikely place: the toothbrush aisle at his local drug store.

For decades, toothbrushes had been, well, toothbrushes---differentiated mainly by minor innovations like bigger brush heads, softer bristles and angled handles. But an expanded array of very high-end electric toothbrushes had recently hit stores. The result was an oddly segmented market: Consumers could choose between plain-Jane toothbrushes costing at most $3 or $4 each, or advanced electric brushes with sonic vibrating bristles retailing for somewhere around $100.

Osher wondered why there wasn't an in-between option.

One of his biggest hits up to that time had been the manufacture and sale of a line of motorized lollipops called SpinPops. From that experience, Osher knew a thing or two about how to make an inexpensive, battery-powered spinning mechanism, and he thought he saw an opportunity.

He leveraged his technical experience, using it to develop and manufacture low- to mid-range electric toothbrushes selling for around $8 or $9 in stores. His new company became very successful, and it was eventually bought by Proctor and Gamble for $475 million. So, if you've ever bought and used one of those disposable $8 electric toothbrushes, you have John Osher to thank---the man who took what he'd learned in creating the battery-powered tooth decay industry and used it to create battery-powered tooth care.

There aren't that many players in the dental care market, and frankly it doesn't seem like there were a lot of entrepreneurs crazy enough to go up against industry giants like Procter & Gamble. But the result is instructive: When you're looking at a business model that seems to work for others and trying to find an opportunity, do what baseball great Willie Keeler once advised: "Hit 'em where they ain't." Keep in mind that the sweet spot might well be the underserved middle of the market.

HIGH-END PRODUCTS

For all the opportunity that can be found in low- and middle-range products and services, many entrepreneurs instinctively look for opportunity on the high end. After all, higher end products can generate wider profit margins while fulfilling more sophisticated customer needs. Without that kind of mindset and aspiration, what progress would there be? Perhaps no innovations have more potential for the kind of creative destruction that would have gotten Joseph Schumpeter excited than the wildly ambitious ones that often characterize high end products. Today, electric vehicles and private space travel spring to mind as ambitious attempts to develop innovative high-end products.

However, while emerging technology and high end products can be a good place to look, they often come fully equipped with serious business and technical risks. Entrepreneurs at the high end often get so excited about technology that they forget to work toward solving a genuine *customer pain*, which we'll explore in-depth in the next module. As an entrepreneur examining new technologies, train yourself to ask: *Is there truly a sustainable demand for this innovation? Could I provide it efficiently, consistently, and profitably?*

When high-end products work, they can provide both tangible value to customers---the utility of the products themselves---and intangible value, such as the benefits of feeling cool, innovative, smart and in style. However, they also require high startup costs, which means you can spend a lot just to learn if the business has a shot at working.

True, those same start-up costs can also serve as barriers to entry and effective defenses against competitors, but they also make it really hard to test ideas before launching. For example, is there really and truly a sustainable demand for electric high-performance vehicles like the ones Tesla Motors develops? Are we at the point where there is sustainable demand for private space launches, like the services offered by SpaceX (cargo) and Virgin Galactic (human passengers)? Those companies are already several years old, and the fact that we can't answer these questions definitively might give you pause, even if in the long run the answer turns out to be a resounding yes.

It's also worth noting that all three of those companies were founded by entrepreneurs who had already enjoyed huge success in other ventures. These entrepreneurs are experienced and savvy, and they can access extensive resources. First-time entrepreneurs should think long and hard before attempting anything so complex.

This doesn't mean you should *always* stay far away, but entering a high-end market requires you to be utterly realistic in assessing your personal strengths and abilities. Do you truly have a unique insight that might give you an advantage in coming up with a high-end product or service? High-end products typically require both promise and credibility---a "big story" and effective marketing along with a technically advanced, sophisticated product. That means that deep industry knowledge becomes even more important. If you want to start an upscale cupcake company in a new city, perhaps you can do so even if you've never worked in a bakery. But if you want to launch a new electric car company like Tesla Motors, you'll be a lot better off if it matches your experience. You'll also likely need large amounts of capital just to test your idea and find out of there's any "there" there.

Serving Macro Changes

Americans, Europeans and Japanese are growing older. The Indian and Chinese middle classes are growing. The world is growing more connected, more environmentally conscious and more innovative than ever before. When you think of how the world around you is changing, think of how those changes can mean opportunity for you as an entrepreneur.

For example, consider some of the needs that aging baby boomers develop as the U.S. population shifts towards a higher percentage of older citizens. Possible opportunities include anything that would address people's hopes for financial stability as they live longer, or help them face their fears of disease and aging. How about addressing their need for affirmation that they've lived their lives meaningfully? What products or services does your background lead you to dream up that could help people bond with their children and grandchildren or their needs for recreation and spiritual connection? How could you help them plan for practical needs, such as for legal services, estate planning, employment discrimination, and end-of-life issues?

Chances are you could add another 10 or 20 items to this list. If you can't, ask your parents or other relatives. Start asking questions, and then listen to the answers. We'll bet you'll find an idea or two.

Booms/Busts in Larger Markets

Even if you find a great niche market, there is always a likelihood that established players will move into your field once they see you enjoying success. Top clothing brands, for example might launch a lower-quality line in order to compete with less-expensive, off-brand competitors. You can hedge against this risk to some degree by finding new opportunities that are a bit tangential to a more obvious market and farther afield from the big players' products.

Take the current push toward green tech and clean energy---for example wind farms and turbines. Modern wind turbines are humongous machines, far too large to be transported on standard semi-trailers. Thus, an entire industry has grown up around giant trucks and massive train cars that are big enough to transport the blades and towers. Innovators in this tangential transportation industry don't necessarily care which wind farms make it or don't; they just care that the market itself survives.

Or else, consider Apple's iPod, iPhone, and iPad. Every time Apple or any other big, popular electronics manufacturer comes out with a must-have new product, entire ancillary industries sprout up:

protective cases, "missing manuals," external speakers and better earphones---often produced and sold by independent companies.

THE MOST IMPORTANT IDEA SO FAR

You might have thought up some good ideas even just while reading this book, and that makes this a good time to reemphasize the three most important things to do with promising ideas: *Test them, test them, and test them.*

Leaping before looking hard enough is the most easily avoidable mistake that entrepreneurs make. So while there is value in moving quickly, there's also inestimable value in ensuring that you move quickly in the right direction. If you're creative and driven enough to come up with a great idea, use that same creativity and drive to find ways to test the idea efficiently before you go all-in.

Look for places---online and off---where you can present ideas and ask for feedback. Talk to lots of prospective customers, explore business plan contests and investigate angel investor groups. Don't be shy: As long as you sincerely believe that there is legitimate value in what you're proposing, you're almost morally obligated to reach out and get the feedback you'll need to reduce your risks and improve your odds. Of course the absolute best way to obtain feedback is to try to sell it to paying customers. Make that sale!

Almost no entrepreneur gets things exactly right with their first idea. So isn't it better to gather data early and adjust what you're doing before you invest too much of your time and treasure? Much more about this as we proceed, but for now, let this be your mantra: Obtain *maximum information for minimum cost.*

THE BIG PICTURE

The ability to look at life's frustrations and difficulties and perceive opportunities instead of problems is a learned skill. It can require some mental practice. You don't need to be a beer drinker, however, or a cupcake eater, or a devotee of mid-range electric toothbrushes to understand the big lesson behind these examples: The best new ideas are often hiding in plain sight. Analyze your experiences and understand what drives your passions. This process will very likely inspire some interesting insights.

Consider idea generation in the context of creative destruction. It's almost inevitable that somebody will eventually develop breakthrough new ventures in areas that interest you. Boston Beer Co. upended the way beer is produced and sold in the United States, but of course Jim Koch wasn't the only aspiring entrepreneur out there who wanted to be able to drink something other than light lager in his local watering hole. The technological innovations we've discussed in this module upended the ways people had done things previously, but many of the insights that led to those innovations and ventures seem almost commonplace in retrospect. For that matter, John Osher reorganized the nation's toothbrush aisles, but isn't it likely that if he hadn't chosen to launch his company, somebody else might eventually have figured out that there was a missing link between $3 and $100 toothbrushes?

We hope this is an inspiring example. You don't need to be the most knowledgeable person in a field or the one with the most advanced ideas. You simply have to be the one who recognizes the opportunities, the one who pairs them with other ideas to create something unique and useful. And you need to be the person who actually takes action. When you do so, you both improve the odds you'll be successful and become part of the engine of progress in a free market society.

Of course, behind this notion of entrepreneurship as a social good, there's also the nagging little question of ensuring you'll make money from your great idea. Moreover, how do you stick to our mantra of obtaining *maximum information for minimum cost* while simultaneously determining whether the great business idea you've come up with will truly lead to a profitable venture?

We'll address these questions in detail in the next module, as we explore how to measure the value your venture would offer to a customer, and calculate whether your great idea is likely to yield a profit.

MODULE 3

"I skate to where the puck is going, not where it has been."

— **Wayne Gretzky**

IDEAS PART 2: CUSTOMER PAIN & VALUE PROPOSITION

Brainstorming, identifying and evaluating ideas are just the first steps in your entrepreneurial marathon. In fact, the process usually leads to some tough questions. How do you refine your new venture concept so you know that your products and services will meet the demands of the market? What do you do in those frustrating instances when you believe you've hit on something great but things just aren't working? How can you figure out ahead of time whether customers will find your idea as exciting as you do?

The ultimate answer is always to let the customer be your compass. This means listening actively to the market and learning to make good judgments about what customers want today---but also what they're likely to want by the time you can deliver solutions. Markets are moving targets. Sometimes prospective customers know what they want and will tell you directly. Other times you need to use your detective skills to discover unarticulated customer needs. Like a doctor interviewing a patient, you need to listen to your customers' complaints---but also think more broadly about their likely causes and solutions.

Peter Thiel, the lawyer-turned-serial-entrepreneur who co-founded PayPal (and who later made the first significant investment in Facebook), offers a great example of how to identify the most acute unmet customer needs before customers themselves can articulate them. When he decided to become an entrepreneur, Thiel went through a brainstorming process similar to the methods we've discussed. He found his first promising idea at the crossroads of his libertarian political ideals and his understanding of the kinds of security and communications technologies that were emerging at the time. Thiel especially wanted to develop a product that would empower people to exchange information and money securely, without government interference.

Thiel and his cofounders launched their company in 1998, calling it Fieldlink. They specialized at first in encrypting information on Palm Pilot personal assistant devices, which were popular at the time. The company's technology also allowed users to transfer money securely from one PDA to another via the devices' infrared sensor. Thiel's venture named its flagship product PayPal, and raised its first round of venture capital. An investor beamed $3 million to Thiel's Palm Pilot at the press event they held to mark the milestone. (At a later event, the company hired the actor who had played Mr. Scott on *Star Trek* to be its spokesman and demonstrate the service. He talked about how he'd "beamed people up" on TV and was now excited to beam money in real life.)

PayPal got great news coverage. But there were only about four million Palm Pilot users. True, beaming money from one PDA to another was probably more convenient than traditional ways of sharing money. News articles at the time used the example of friends trying to split a dinner check.

But was it an acute enough pain to build a company around? The world was changing very quickly. Internet commerce was growing exponentially, but the development of easy ways to transfer money between users who were many miles apart hadn't kept up. For example, the user base of the online auction site eBay had nearly quadrupled in a year---from from 2.1 million users in 1998 to 7.7 million users in 1999---and would triple again in 2000. But buyers were still paying for purchases by sending paper checks in the mail.

With its emphasis on in-person transactions, the early news coverage of PayPal made it seem as if the company might have a neat idea that was focused on solving the previous decade's problem.

Fortunately, Thiel, and his cofounder, Max Levchin, had been able to anticipate this new, more deeply felt customer pain long before the customers grew aware of it. Rather than expand the service just to work with cellular phones and pagers, as they'd originally envisioned, they'd decided to enable customers to use the service with just an email address---no handheld device necessary.

That idea, "an afterthought," according to one early employee, eventually defined the company. "Since users of the Palm software would need to upload their encrypted transactions to the PayPal website anyway, Peter, Max, and the development team agreed that it made sense to create an account that could work with or without a Palm."

PayPal switched gears. Things took off. Users signed up by the millions.

Thiel explained to us that figuring out what the market really needs is a never-ending process.

"You need to listen to customers and let them help you," he told us, but the kicker is, "customers don't know exactly what is possible or desirable."

It's up to the innovative outsider---you----to come up with "the kind of thing that customers might need that no one has ever thought of before."

FIND YOUR CUSTOMER'S PAIN

How does an entrepreneur identify what customers will buy before the products or services exist? To answer that question, it helps to address another question first: Why does anybody buy anything? At the most basic level, people typically spend money on two things:

First, they readily spend money to *combat pain*. Second, they spend money to *pursue pleasure*.

We list pain and pleasure in that order for a reason. All things being equal, the more acute the pain or problem, the more likely it is that you'll be able to offer a compelling solution. The more compelling the solution, the more quickly the customer will pay. From an entrepreneur's perspective this means that it's often better to be in a "pain business" than a "pleasure business." There is simply more staying power in pain-solving businesses.

In fact, entrepreneurs often wind up using "customer pain" as a synonym for "customer needs" or "customer problems." At times this can seem a bit over the top, even cynical, as we talk about soothing the customer's pain by selling him an electric gadget or a new style of clothing. But referring to *pain* rather than *needs* or *preferences* reinforces the point: Customers are people. They appreciate the world through the prism of their experiences. They sense what challenges or bothers them (their pain) but they often can't even conceive of the solutions (their needs).

So, look for the pain. Think of things that people find disturbing, frustrating, urgent, or uncomfortable. Then, with the pain clearly recognized and in mind, switch gears and develop cures. Focus on healing. Let that be your guide as you try to invent a venture that will make the pain go away.

There is one more component here. You want to focus not just on identifying what the pain is, but also figuring out *when* people feel it most pressingly. It's almost always easier to sell a solution to a current, intense pain than to solve something less acute. If you've ever had to call a locksmith or a plumber in an emergency, you'll understand this point almost intuitively. It's easier to sell somebody a new car when he or she has just learned that the faithful old clunker will need a $1,500 repair job. It's easier to sell aspirin than vitamins.

Human as this desire to end pain is, the quest applies to business customers, too. Businesses generally strive to do two things: increase sales and cut costs. So, if you can demonstrate new ways that business customers can find new markets, create new products, or even raise prices on existing products, you can solve their pain by helping to increase revenue. If you can offer business customers innovative new ways to manage their workforces, comply with government regulations or build infrastructure, you can solve their pain by helping to cut costs.

One final thing to consider: the customer and the end user are not necessarily the same person. If you sell games and toys for example, often your users might be children, but the customers who actually buy your products are probably their parents. Likewise, if you run an Internet search on Google, you're Google's user, but it's only when you purchase Google AdWords that you become Google's customer.

Would-be social entrepreneurs, especially, should pay attention to this potential difference between users and customers. Suppose you want to try to improve inner city schools, or combat a disease, or bring clean drinking water to a part of the world that needs it. In these cases, the students, patients, or other people you're trying to help will be your users, but the donors who you hope will fund your venture are the customers. So be sure to look for the pain that potential donors feel---be it a sense of altruism, a desire for fulfillment, guilt, or something else---and find compelling solutions. Your organization exists in order to solve your users' need, but it's the manner in which you solve your donors' pain that creates a going concern.

HOW THINGS PAID OFF FOR PAYPAL

The PayPal story is instructive for at least one other reason. For every new customer who used PayPal, a few potential new PayPal customers were born. People who had never imagined sending money via email suddenly had new pain as they learned for the first time that it was possible. They received emails saying that there was cold, hard cash waiting for them. They wanted the money and the only way to get it was to sign up for PayPal.

"The value increased as more people used it," Thiel described to us. "PayPal is more valuable with 100 million people than with 100,000 people."

The proof is in these numbers. Once PayPal adapted its product, the user base increased rapidly. In its early days, the company actually paid users $10 or $20 to get them to sign up, but soon PayPal was exceeding its rosiest user projections by a factor of 40. Within a year, they were up to 7 million. Less than two years after that, eBay bought the company for $1.5 billion.

Thiel personally took home about $60 million. He went on to become a hugely successful investor in Facebook and other companies. He's since run a large hedge fund, started an innovative venture capital fund and launched several other interesting new firms. He was also flat-out hooked on the process of creative destruction.

"Fundamentally, I enjoy the process of working with other talented people to start and build business," he explained. "The biggest way that one can impact the world---the most underrated way to change the world---is to start a new company."

TESTING FOR CUSTOMER PAIN

There's a simple method for figuring out whether your new venture idea will address a real customer pain. It comes down to this: *Can you describe the pain your company solves---and why anyone should care---in just a few words? Can you then persuade a prospective customer to purchase your product using your simple explanation?*

If so, congratulations. You're miles ahead of most entrepreneurs. Innovators and founders who need paragraphs to describe their market or persuade potential customers demonstrate that they haven't refined their businesses sufficiently.

This works in reverse as well. Think of the some of the most successful companies in the world and also of some of the companies we've used as examples already. For the truly great ones, you can probably describe very quickly what they do and thus what customer pain they exist to solve. Apple exists because *people want elegant technology.* Google exists because *advertisers want to reach customers effectively.* Starbucks exists because *people are addicted to caffeine.*

Dr. John Osher's Spinbrush toothbrush? *People want clean teeth.* (Or perhaps more simply: *People want teeth!*). Zipcar? *People want easy, convenient transportation.* As for Boston Beer Company, it might be that people want good beer---or else, maybe it's something they're less likely to articulate, like that they want to be perceived as more sophisticated drinkers.

Is it fatal if you can't articulate a compelling customer pain? It can be eventually, but it also simply means that you haven't fully formed your new venture idea yet. Many great entrepreneurs go through numerous iterations before they figure out the best uses for their innovations. It can take time to find the pain.

BUSINESS EXAMPLE:
FINDING CUSTOMER PAIN

A small manufacturing firm called Louis J. Hansen Enterprises sits near an overpass in the Chicago suburb of Cicero, Illinois. The company's eponymous and highly skilled founder has worked there for decades building the company into something special. Hansen holds several patents, including a method of aligning grinding wheels precisely enough to refine and polish the fan blades on jet airplane engines. As a result, tiny Hansen Enterprises soon counted some of the world's biggest aviation manufacturers among its customers. That's a limited market, however. After Hansen saturated it and made a small profit, he didn't find many other applications. He had developed sophisticated technology and solved an important customer pain, but it was a pain felt by a small set of customers.

About 400 miles to the northwest, two hockey players, brothers Scott and Brennan Olson, found an old, experimental pair of inline roller skates in a used sporting goods store. Inspired by the design, they played around with different improvements of their own, and stumbled onto a similar method of aligning wheels in a row. They offered homemade inline skates to their hockey friends, incorporated their new company, which they called Rollerblade, and enjoyed brisk sales---at least for a company that they ran entirely out of their parents' basement. By the early 1980s, thousands of serious hockey players in the U.S. and Canada were training on Rollerblades.

The Olsons sold their company in 1984, and the new buyers saw even greater potential. The company now focused its efforts on Miami Beach, Florida and Venice Beach, California, where they gave away inline skates and tried to build Rollerblades into an exercise phenomenon. The plan worked. People who had never seen a hockey game or tried on ice skates were soon working up a sweat while Rollerblading on city streets worldwide. Today, more than 30 million people own a pair of Rollerblades or similar inline skates.

Here's the thing: both these businesses revolved (literally) around almost identical technological innovations. Whether you're polishing airplane parts, training for hockey in the off-season, or working out on the Venice boardwalk, the key is figuring out how to keep a series of rubber wheels balanced perfectly even when they're spinning at high speed for a long time. By focusing on different customer needs (everything from the need to build safe airplanes to the personal desire to get in shape and look good while doing it) with similar products, each entrepreneur reached a different level of success.

The moral of the story is that it pays to solve the *broadest* pain possible. If you're convinced you've come up with a great innovation, keep thinking of who else's pain you might be able to solve with it. Find the most intense, acute pain that your product or service can relieve. That's the one to build a great company around.

FIND NEW CUSTOMER PAIN

The process of creative destruction often leads to the creation of new customer pain. For example, nobody needed an auto mechanic until entrepreneurs started building cars. Nobody needed identity theft protection or credit monitoring until entrepreneurs created the personal credit report to address problems in lending and borrowing money.

Apple first unveiled the iPod during the heyday of Napster, when people could share songs with each other for free via the Internet. Yet consumers' widespread adoption of the product confirmed for Apple a new, unmet need: Customers wanted to be able to get music quickly, easily, relatively cheaply, and perhaps most importantly, *legally*. The result was iTunes, which grew into one of Apple's most successful products.

At the same time, Apple designed the iPod so that it could be used only with headphones (earbuds, in the company's nomenclature). Users had a great new way to transport and play music but no way to play it loud enough to share. They developed new pain, and many other companies developed complementary products like external speakers and docking stations that offered solutions.

So pay attention to trends and innovations, but don't be like the hordes of other would-be entrepreneurs who rush to market with "me-too" products. Look instead for the new pain each entrepreneur causes, even as he provides a solution to something else. You're almost guaranteed to find something. Customer pain is the ultimate renewable resource.

IDENTIFY INTANGIBLE NEEDS

Many customer needs are for things the customers themselves don't fully understand or articulate. Why buy an iPod instead of a less expensive MP3 player? Why drive a Lexus instead of a Toyota? Why pick one brand of artificially sweetened carbonated beverage over another one? Usually the answers to these questions have less to do with features than with image, feelings, and intangibles.

Clothing retailer Abercrombie and Fitch generated revenue of about $3.5 billion in 2010. The company has its roots in a 100-year-old sporting goods store. What sets it apart from its competitors so that they can charge a huge premium for their clothes? The answer is that they don't sell clothes as much as a lifestyle and a promise. Walk by the store, and you'll see massive posters of beautiful, scantily clothed young people, reinforcing an image. All this time you thought you needed diet and exercise to look great? They're driving home the message that what you really need is a pair of $120 jeans and a $70 t-shirt.

It's easy to become a cynic when we look at intangible needs as part of customer pain. Sure, some intangible needs can seem silly, but many others are legitimate, even vital. Sometimes as an entrepreneur, these are the most intense kinds of pain you can address.

VALUE PROPOSITION: SOLVE CUSTOMER PAIN PROFITABLY

So, you've brainstormed an idea and you have a sense of the customer pain your product can solve. The next step in your billion-dollar-business generating process is to figure out if you can fill that need profitably. You'll want to estimate the economics as best you can, so as to figure out ahead of time if customers will actually agree to purchase your product or service for significantly more than it costs you to produce it. You need to understand the *value proposition* you're creating. It's comprised of three factors: ***Production cost:*** What will it cost you to develop and produce your product or service?

Customer utility: What dollar amount can you use to represent the degree to which your customer will value the product?

Price: How much will your customer be willing to pay?

It's pretty simple: the lower your production costs and the higher the customer utility, the better the value proposition. You want to create and capture as much value as possible. To take a pretty straightforward example, suppose we wanted to calculate a value proposition for a cup of coffee---more specifically, for a grande soy latte at Starbucks. We'd need to estimate each of the three numbers so that we can plug them into the three parts of the framework.

We'd begin with ***production cost***, which is often the number you can estimate with the most precision. If you're planning to sell lattes, hopefully you can figure out how much it costs to make them. Likewise, if you're planning to manufacture electronics, bake cupcakes, or develop games that run on social networking websites, hopefully you know enough to come up with some kind of estimate of what it will cost you to produce them. If not, then it's time to do some research and figure it out. In this case, you'd probably have direct costs, such as the cost of beans, soy milk, paper cups and those little corrugated cardboard sleeves so your customers' hands won't burn. You'd also have indirect costs: things like the tables and chairs you need to furnish the store and the marketing campaigns that plug into peoples' intangible needs and make grande soy lattes seem like a desirable drink.

So, what are the true production costs for a single grande soy latte at Starbucks? Let's use reasonable estimates here, because Starbucks CEO Howard Schultz isn't likely to share the exact data with us. However, we can make an educated guess---something you'd be doing as an entrepreneur in any event. Based on our research and interviews, let's say it probably costs cost Starbucks about $1.75 to produce each latte.

That's step one. Step two is to figure out the *customer utility*. In other words, what is a single cup of this piping hot beverage actually worth to a customer? This is a more complicated estimate. There are probably dozens of different customer utilities here, because there are dozens of different types of customers. The utility to a mildly curious Starbucks customer who has never before tried a soy latte (and who therefore doesn't know what he's missing) isn't all that high. Maybe he or she would be willing to spend a couple of bucks, just once, out of curiosity. The utility to a true caffeine addict is higher. He or she literally feels pain without a daily dose of the stimulant. Maybe he or she would be willing to spend three times as much as the latte neophyte.

Again, in order to come up with some well-considered estimates, there is no substitute for research. One simple answer might be to start asking potential customers what they think about lattes and other similar drinks. You could look at what similar drinks sell for elsewhere. You could do interviews and conduct focus groups. Offer pre-sale deals and see what level people bite at. The key is to use several different strategies, and see if you get consistent results. Since we're plugging in numbers here, for purposes of this example let's say the average utility to a Starbucks customer would be $5. (Notice that we're not yet concerned with how many potential customers there might be---we'll get to that. For now, we just want to know: if you're the kind of person who likes grande soy lattes, what are they worth to you on average?)

So we have an estimated $1.75 production cost, and an estimated $5 customer utility. Those are pretty promising numbers, and they lead us directly to the last estimate: What is the *optimal price*?

Determining how to price products optimally is a never-ending challenge. Often you'll cycle through several different pricing experiments before you figure out what works best. Usually---not always, but usually---what you'd think happens, happens: The higher the price, the lower the demand. The key to keep in mind, of course, is that the purchase price you set must be somewhere *between* what it costs you (or Starbucks) to produce the latte and the utility to the customer. Obvious as this concept seems when we write it here in black and white, a lot of smart, talented entrepreneurs aren't able to maintain this balance. Of course we don't need to estimate pricing strategy in the case of Starbucks since we can walk to nearly any urban street corner in America and find out: $3.85, give or take.

Two more points to consider: the *value created* and *value captured*. If Starbucks produces lattes at $1.75, and the average utility to your customers is $5, then they've created $3.25 of value. And if they're selling lattes at $3.85, then they are *capturing* $2.10 of value. This example shows a pretty well balanced value proposition at Starbucks, and perhaps helps to explain why the company's stores remain popular and profitable. At least in this example, based on reasonable assumptions, Starbucks creates significant value for the customer, and it also captures a sizeable portion of that value for itself. Pretty smart.

So, why even bother with the exercise of calculating a value proposition? Two reasons, actually. First, the process helps you diagnose quickly whether you're on to something promising and potentially profitable. Second, it shows where you need to focus your efforts to improve a marginal business idea. It makes it easier to identify where the problems truly lie before you get started:

- If your customer utility and your production costs are both high, for example, then you might need to focus your efforts on reducing your costs. Are you including additional features that your customers don't find useful? Are there less expensive materials you could use without sacrificing quality? Is there a way you can reach customers more efficiently?

- If customer utility and production costs are both low, you might focus your efforts on finding different customers for whom your product might have a higher utility. Can you find customers with more pressing needs? Is there a way to make your product better without spending much more money? Is there a way to convince existing customers to use your product more often, so they might buy more replacements?

- Finally, if costs are low while utility is high, you could focus on how much you can increase the asking price---and thus put you in a position to capture more value. You'll make more money, of course, and you'll also build a more interesting, stable, and rewarding business.

Again, these concepts start to seem obvious after we've explored them a bit. They're simple math, really: What will it cost you to produce the product? What will the utility be to your customers? What should the price be, and how much value can you capture? And yet, most entrepreneurs never set out to examine any of these calculations until deep in the game. Remember, PayPal had to retool its product---and by implication, its value proposition---before it could survive and thrive. Even Robin Chase at Zipcar realized after launching that she'd miscalculated her value proposition by underestimating her production costs. Fortunately her customers found Zipcar provided such a high utility that there was room to increase the price, otherwise the company would have been doomed.

These are things that people need to think about---before they open a store, before they renovate a restaurant, before they invest their life savings or mortgage their house and before they try to get others to invest. Only the most fortunate figure it out soon enough to do something about it.

How Value Propositions Evolve Over Time

Like markets, value propositions change over time---sometimes a very short time. Here's an example. The *New York Times* was once America's undisputed paper of record, and it provided a very high utility to its customers (readers and advertisers alike). If something wasn't in the *Times*, the saying went, it just hadn't happened. Now, however, there are so many competing news sources that the average customer utility of the *Times* has almost certainly fallen. Meanwhile, production costs have risen. The paper has struggled with how to make money on the Internet, launching new iterations of *Times Select* over the years and increasing its cover price twofold in the space of 24 months. It looks at present as if the company is probably capturing almost all of the value it is creating.

Meanwhile, look at the value propositions offered by other modern information services, for example, Craigslist and AOL's Huffington Post. Both have grown exponentially. Neither charges its users for most services. Production costs are comparatively tiny, as it turns out that there are millions of users who want to run classified ads or even write articles for free. The customer utility doesn't have to be very high when both costs and price are low.

THE BIG PICTURE

Graduating from the brainstorming process to the practice of actually finding customer pain and calculating a value proposition means you're moving from the realm of the entrepreneurial dreamers to the doers. By applying rigorous analysis to your ideas, you're greatly improving the odds that those you decide to pursue will prove worthwhile. It's not coming up with one great idea that makes an entrepreneur. Instead, it's having the courage to reject many interesting ideas before identifying and pursuing the most promising of them.

This distinction also starts to make a difference in the context of creative destruction. Professor Schumpeter didn't create a rubric that leaves us carte blanche to simply throw rocks in a pond and see where the ripples lead. Instead, as entrepreneurs, we embrace the calling to act both boldly and ethically to improve peoples' lives. It's a tough challenge to take on, but at its core, it's a chance to be the kind of forward-thinking leader who thinks up solutions before the rest of the world even realizes there are problems.

You're also hereby granted a license to make mistakes, as long as you don't insist on making the same ones over and over again.

That's simply how this works. PayPal wouldn't have survived if Peter Thiel and his colleagues hadn't looked ahead, retooled their original plan and changed the company's focus to online transactions. Zipcar would have failed if Robin Chase hadn't recalculated her value proposition.

As long as you're willing to keep listening, watching, and predicting what your customers will need, you're doing the right thing when you pivot in response to the market. You're increasing your odds of success and of feeling the intense satisfaction that derives from helping even one customer to address his needs and end his pain.

Of course, let's be honest: you're not in this to help just one customer. You're in it to help as many customers as possible, and to create as successful and impactful a new venture as you can. This means tailoring your product idea so that it will reach the largest possible market---and that's a process we'll explore in the next module.

MODULE 4

"Test fast, fail fast, adjust fast."

– Tom Peters

IDEAS PART 3: MAXIMUM INFORMATION
FOR MINIMUM COST

Life is short. You only get a limited number of chances and you can only spend limited resources. As an entrepreneur, you want to do everything you can to separate the fantastic ideas from the fool's gold. That's why it's so important to embrace the principle you've seen repeated throughout this book: *Get maximum information for minimum cost.*

Robin Wolaner, who started *Parenting* magazine with a $5,000 initial investment and built it into a publishing success story with a circulation of two million, offers an excellent example of how this is done.

Wolaner had worked in publishing since graduating from college in the mid-1970s, starting as a secretary and copywriter at *Penthouse*, where she came up with the magazine's slogan: "More than just a pretty face." She eventually moved on to *Runners World* and then became the publisher of the nonprofit liberal magazine *Mother Jones*, while simultaneously teaching courses on publishing to supplement her income. During that time, Wolaner was constantly thinking about new audiences to target and new magazines to start. Though she was not a parent herself, she realized that as more of her generational peers had children, there might be an opportunity for her.

"I had three pregnant women on my very small staff," Wolaner told us. "My head of circulation was one of the mothers, and I asked her, 'So, now that you're a mother, what magazine do you read?"

Basically, Wolaner's colleague answered, nothing---and not for lack of looking. Someone had given her a subscription to the category-leading title, *Parents*, but it seemed old and stodgy, nothing she was really interested in. Wolaner knew about a publishing entrepreneur who had launched an upscale, even glamorous magazine called *American Health*, and was enjoying success. If they can launch something like that in the health category, Wolaner thought, we can do it in the parenting category. She realized she had likely discovered an important, simple, urgent customer pain---something like, *people want to be good parents*---or else, *moms and dads are afraid they'll screw up their kids.*

From her industry experience, Wolaner figured she'd need to raise about $5 million to launch the magazine. She'd never tried to raise so much as a penny before. Nevertheless, she met a venture capitalist who liked the idea and who quickly gave her $5,000 in what he called, "walking around money" to get started. However, he insisted that she conduct an ambitious direct-mail market test before raising the money to start the magazine for real.

Wolaner hated this idea at first, especially because she figured it would require spending $100,000 that she didn't actually have, but she agreed nevertheless. She convinced a direct-mail guru she'd met to help her assemble 27 different mailing lists, from which they identified pregnant women and parents of small children across the United States. Meanwhile, she worked with a designer to put together a mockup of what the cover of her magazine might look like and a marketing package.

All told, they sent 130,000 mailings, divided into three groups. One group of recipients was asked if they'd be willing to subscribe to the new *Parenting* magazine for $12 a year. A second group was asked if they'd be willing to subscribe for $15 a year. The third group was also asked if they would subscribe for $15 a year, but the wording of the marketing piece made it sound more like a binding contract than a mere expression of interest.

The response was overwhelming---and a great success. Wolaner had been aiming for a reply rate between 3.5 and 5 percent; the actual results were close to 7 percent. Regardless of whether she asked for $12 or $15, the parents bought into the idea of *Parenting*. This relatively inexpensive test proved that there was a big market and provided valuable pricing information.

But, the process is not always easy. When we talked with Wolaner, in fact, she recoiled at the idea that things had gone smoothly and stress-free.

"That's not what happened," she insisted. "I had my maximum information but I maxed out my credit cards."

Not only that, but raising the money for the direct mail test was an intense and traumatic experience. She didn't put the last of the funding in place until just a week before the envelopes had to go out.

That said, Wolaner proved the demand for her proposed product on a budget that was just a tiny fraction of the $5 million she'd sought to start the magazine itself. She had the data she needed to prove demand and a key, provable insight into the market's size. She obtained *maximum information for minimum cost* and proved the attractiveness of the business she wanted to build. That made all the difference as she raised more money, launched the publication, and grew to dominate the category.

THE PROCESS SO FAR

Before we go any deeper into the process, let's briefly review the systemic approach we've been describing to develop and test a great business idea. There are really four phases of idea generation: brainstorming (which we covered in Module 2), identifying customer pain and calculating a value proposition (which we covered in Module 3) and proving market demand (which we'll discuss in this module).

In practice, you will likely cycle through these steps, proceeding through multiple iterations, honing your thinking and ideas. You'll think of an idea but perhaps find that it doesn't really solve a customer pain. Still, that process might lead you to think more about the potential customer you'd hoped to reach, and lead you to think about what your potential customer does in fact spend money on. Since figuring out what the customer finds useful is a fundamental component of calculating a value proposition, that might in turn lead you to brainstorm yet another idea, and so on.

Moreover, just to add one more variable to the mix, this is all a perpetual process, designed to last long after you've launched your new venture. You might well look back a year or two into your business and realize that the ultimate model you've created varies significantly from your original plan. Getting the data that guides you is critical, and yet as an entrepreneur, you will almost never have enough time or money. So, what's the answer?

All together now. It's critically important: *maximum information for minimum cost.*

HOW BIG IS THE MARKET?

Robin Wolaner eventually launched *Parenting* as a joint venture with Time Inc., which had planned to launch its own magazine for Baby Boomer parents but heard about her efforts. She was simply much farther along than they were.

Notwithstanding Wolaner's happy result, the truth is that entrepreneurs tend to be overly optimistic when they calculate market size. An important discipline for an entrepreneur is to aim high while remaining reasonably pragmatic. Targeting a $500 million market and learning that it's only 10 percent as large as you thought is better than targeting a $1 million market and being right. This leads us to the commonly used 10 percent rule: *only assume you'll capture 10 percent of any market, especially as a first-time entrepreneur.* You might get lucky and exceed that level but luck is not a plan. Besides, the concept of creative destruction reminds us that even if you are successful, other entrepreneurs will enter and capture part of the market, too. Just as we're advising you to model and copy success, others will copy your success. In the long run, a small number of companies will likely dominate a new market. However, in the medium term, competition is virtually guaranteed. You need to develop a plan for short- and medium- term success, which can lead to long-term dominance. In order to do that, you need to understand the opportunities of a new, dynamic, and untested market.

That said, markets *are* quantifiable. As you attempt to predict market share, begin by thinking about these three factors:

- First, what size is the total potential market?

- Second, what is the likely adoption rate of the new product, and the total addressable market (TAM)?

- Third, how many potential users will you eventually convert?

Calculating Total Potential Market

Let's return to our cupcake bakery example to explain how this is done. Let's say you wanted to spread the New York City gourmet cupcake trend to the good people of Omaha, Nebraska. In order to figure out the first component---*total potential market*---you might start off with the city's estimated population, which was about 438,000 in 2008, according to the U.S. Census Bureau.

As always, the keys to finding these figures are research and assertiveness. The information is usually out there somewhere, ripe for the (ethical) taking. You might flat-out ask the owners of traditional bakeries for their opinions---or even better, for their hard sales data. You might be surprised at how much they'll share with you. Alternatively, you might call the suppliers you'll be using and ask them for estimates. You could figure out how many bakeries exist already in Omaha, estimate how much business each one does, and work out the math that way. Or else you might look to other cities and try to find out how many cupcakes their bakeries sell. The bottom line is that you want to be creative and find multiple methods to estimate this information.

Suppose, based on your research, you conclude that on average perhaps 1 in 9 of those 438,000 Omahans is likely to buy at least one dessert serving---not necessarily a cupcake, just a dessert of some sort---from a local bakery every two weeks. That would give you about 48,666 bakery customers (438,000 population divided by 9). If you estimate that this group probably spends an average of $10 on each purchase, and do a little more simple math, you can come up with about a $12,653,160-a-year bakery dessert market in Omaha (*48,666 customers x $10 x 26 weeks=$12,653,160*).

Maybe you can make a compelling case that New York-style cupcakes will prove so trendy and be so popular in Omaha that the market is even bigger, but for simplicity's sake, let's go with a total potential market of $12.5 million.

ADOPTION RATE AND TOTAL ADDRESSABLE MARKET (TAM)

Great, step one is done. Next, you'll need to figure out the likely adoption rate within that potential market. In other words, how many of those nearly 48,666 dessert aficionados will abandon their sweet treat of choice and prefer your gourmet cupcakes? Again, you'll want to beg, borrow, and do everything short of steal to get the data you need to figure this one out. You might run a focus group, interview prospective customers outside an existing bakery or even set up shop for a couple of days on a street corner, selling or giving away sample cupcakes and gauging peoples' reactions. Maybe you'd find it's useful to extrapolate the degree to which other coastal trends have caught on among Omahans.

Alternatively, as a starting point, you might look at the success that gourmet cupcakes have had in other cities. Let's say for argument's sake that on the high end, you find that 70 percent of dessert aficionados in New York City purchase gourmet cupcakes and on the low end, 26 percent of hard-core bakery lovers in Los Angeles are adopting the product. Regardless, you're looking for reasonable good faith projections---and to get as close to the honest truth as possible. You'll never get the exact number, but that's okay. Remember, you are calculating a range and it's not going to be exact. It's better to be approximately right, rather than precisely wrong.

In this case, we might apply the numbers like so: At best, you'll find a high, New York-style, 70 percent adoption rate. Seventy percent of $12.5 million is $8.75 million. On the low end, you might get a lower, L.A.-style adoption rate of as little as 26 percent of that same $12.5 million, which comes out to $3.25 million. Notice that what we've really done here is refine the potential market to more precisely estimate the total addressable market; that is how much revenue the "Omaha gourmet cupcake industry" can generate.

PROJECTED CUSTOMER CAPTURE

Not too bad, you might think, between $3.25 million and $8.75 million in cupcakes! This leads to the final calculation: What percentage of that estimated market will *you* be able to capture? If you were the only gourmet cupcake vendor in Omaha, and you offered a great product and great service with a fun marketing campaign, you might well be in a position to capture a significant chunk of that market. But, remember, entrepreneurs often overestimate both market size and the portion of that market that they'll be able to capture. If you're successful, and you start selling a lot of cupcakes, rest assured that others will enter the market to compete.

As you make this final calculation, remember you're not just trying to figure out how much of the market you can capture when you're the only game in town. You want to figure out the *competitive state*---the percentage you'll capture as other players join the field. This is the point where you might apply the 10 percent rule. Maybe you'll exceed one-tenth of the market, but it's dangerous to assume so early on. Again, as a failsafe, especially as a first-time entrepreneur, it's best to be confident that you're in a venture that can survive even as a 10 percent player.

So to complete our estimation of the Omaha cupcake market, a new entrepreneur capturing 10 percent of the market could expect to gross between $325,000 and $875,000 in revenue. Of course, estimates of expenses and profitability are important too. They are initially understood through the value proposition calculation, and later through more complete financial modeling. For now, however, it appears that there might be enough revenue to support a specialty cupcake shop in Omaha.

Market Size Recap

Market size estimation is really important. It's worth us running through another example just to ensure it all makes sense. It's relatively easy---and yet, comparatively few entrepreneurs actually do this simple math ahead of time. It's a very common reason for their ultimate failure. In fact, it's almost a cliché among professional investors that entrepreneurs think their ideas are so impressive that the *total addressable market* amounts to "everybody." Entrepreneurs don't know the steps involved in estimating markets, so they throw out wild guesses: *If we can just get one percent of mothers under 40---or else, vegetarians* or *middle-class Indians to buy the product*, these entrepreneurs posit, *we'll all be rich.* As you can imagine, without some rigor going into the estimate, it's difficult to convince investors to back your venture---and good for them!

For argument's sake, let's take a look at what John Osher might well have gone through as he figured out the market for his mid-range, battery-operated toothbrushes.

First, calculate the *total potential market* for American mid-range battery powered toothbrushes. At the time when Osher launched his company, let's assume there were about 250 million Americans of tooth-brushing age. If we assume that each one bought six toothbrushes a year on average, at an average price of $3 each, we'd wind up with a $4.5 billion total potential market. (250,000,000 people x 6 toothbrushes x $3).

Second, figure out the likely adoption rate for mid-range battery-powered brushes. To keep things simple, let's say Osher figured out that about 12.5 percent of Americans on the whole were likely to set aside their low-tech manual toothbrushes and use a battery-powered, spinning version per year. How might he have come to that conclusion? Again, maybe he ran focus groups. Maybe he looked at adoption rates for new mid-range products in other health and beauty categories. Remember, this isn't an exact science. Maybe customers would buy more than one mid-range electric toothbrush a year. Maybe there would be room to raise prices. Regardless, that 12.5 percent seems reasonable, and it amounts to a predicted $562.5 million total addressable market.

Finally, how much of that market was Osher likely to capture? Maybe he hoped that in the first few months he'd capture 80 or 90 percent as he'd be the only manufacturer of any consequence trying to make and sell mid-range electric toothbrushes. But he was smart enough to recognize that if the market proved robust, giants like Procter & Gamble and Johnson & Johnson would compete with their own versions. Other small start-ups might also try to imitate his success. At the very best, Osher might have hoped to capture somewhere between 40 and 50 percent of the market once things settled out. Split the difference, and maybe he was looking at 45 percent of $562.5 million, or roughly $253 million. (Apply the 10 percent rule to that $562.5 million market, and Osher would have projected nearly $56 million a year, which is still quite interesting.)

As it happens, Osher's company sold roughly $200 million worth of SpinBrushes, a stunning success.

AVOIDING POOR OPPORTUNITIES

Sometimes the math just doesn't work. Suppose, for example, that you examined the New York City cupcake craze but decided you were too late for that party, and instead looked for other trends that hadn't yet migrated to other places. As a result, you might consider chopped salad restaurants, which as we write seem to be very popular in the Big Apple.

As you examine the market, you might make some interesting observations: People generally buy salads when they're about to eat them. They're not necessarily eager for them for them all day long. Run through the numbers and you might conclude that the total addressable market for chopped salad restaurants isn't the same as the total addressable market for all restaurants, or else for food in general. Chopped salad restaurants likely see a lot of demand at lunchtime if things go well, perhaps from about 11:30 a.m. to 1:30 p.m. each day---but if that's the scope of your busy time, you're only really selling your product for 10 or 14 hours a week. Suddenly, chopped salads seem like a less promising business, especially with multiple competitors. Perhaps the business works well in very dense urban areas, but just wouldn't make economic sense in a suburban community.

Market size calculations like these can quickly help transform gut feelings to hard data. (In the case of calorie-laden cupcakes, maybe it's a *straight-to-the-gut* feeling.) Enough people like sweet, trendy things that, at a quick glance, it sort of makes sense that cupcakes (and toothbrushes for that matter) should find footholds. Chopped salads, on the other hand, just "feel" a little more regional. Are similar percentages of Omahans and New Yorkers eager to set aside sandwiches and meat dishes for salads?

The point of this calculation, however---in fact, the point of this book---is to move away from gut feelings and toward as much hard data as possible. The more you can do so and the earlier you can do it, the better your odds of finding the right idea that will bring you success as an entrepreneur.

SCALABILITY

There's another concept to consider when you're examining market size: *scalability*.

It might seem obvious that new ventures want to grow, but unmanaged growth can kill a business quickly. So, to the maximum extent you can, you want to explore: how well does your business scale? If you predict conservative growth and you're surprised by high demand, that's often a happy outcome. Importantly though, as you grow bigger, will your gross and net margins increase? Or does getting bigger actually cost you money?

Scalability depends in large part on the relative levels of fixed costs and variable costs. For instance, Microsoft's core business is highly scalable. Having spent the money to develop and market the latest edition of Microsoft Office, as an example, each additional copy of the program costs the company only a few dollars to produce, and yet they're able to set a retail price around $400. But take another very successful company in a different industry: Honda Motor Company has huge fixed costs in its automobile business. It often costs hundreds of millions of dollars to design, manufacture, and market cars, even before the first customer gets his keys and inhales that new car smell. Moreover, the variable costs are high as well---literally tons of material, many man-hours of labor, and high transportation costs are required for each unit.

Comparatively, the auto industry isn't very scalable at all. Profit margins are low on each car, so the keys to success include volume, mass customization, and focusing as much effort as possible on a few high-margin products.

Train yourself to think this way, and predicting scalability with some accuracy becomes almost automatic. PayPal? Fixed costs in designing the system were high, but the cost of adding each new customer is almost nothing: highly scalable. Gourmet cupcakes? The investment in retail space and baking equipment might be substantial to start but each additional cupcake doesn't cost that much to bake. Moderately scalable.

Yet think about some of the businesses that we see people start every day in America, often to less-than optimal results. People who launch restaurants or service businesses, from law firms to barber shops, often have significant fixed costs---long-term leases and tens or hundreds of thousands of dollars in education and certifications, for example. But there are only so many hours that can be billed, and only so many seats in a restaurant. Adding people and space can mean high variable costs as well. There might be some appealing things about those industries, but scalability often isn't one of them.

BUSINESS EXAMPLE:
MAXIMUM INFORMATION FOR MINIMUM COST

Two Parisians we'll call Henri and Jean had the same business idea at the same time. They were both accomplished chocolatiers working in a bakery, and several customers had urged each of them to open their own shops. A few even offered to back them in business.

Henri found an appealing retail space that had just become available on a busy street in a trendy area. He signed a lease on the store. A few of the customers who had encouraged him backed off when it was time to actually invest, but Henri made up the difference from his personal savings and on his credit cards. He didn't have an unlimited budget, but he was able to spend many thousands of dollars to build out an appealing store, print marketing materials and hire staff. He opened for business, proud and excited, utterly convinced that his chocolates would sell.

Jean moved more cautiously. He found a temporarily empty store about a mile away from Henri, negotiated a two-month starter lease, and spent little on renovations. He hung heavy velvet curtains, and scrounged some glass display cases and lighting that a jewelry store had left over when they'd remodeled. Things looked as nice as possible given his tight budget.

Fast-forward a few weeks: *Zut alors!* It turned out that running a high-end chocolate shop was much harder than either entrepreneur envisioned.

Jean concluded at the end of his two-month lease that the market for $5 and $8 chocolates was limited. He closed the store. He had suffered a loss, but not a catastrophic one--a few months of time, and a few rent payments---and he was quickly able to get another job as a baker while he contemplated his next move. Henri, on the other hand, was in a much tougher situation. He'd committed himself to the lease and had much higher startup costs. Eight months into the venture he wound up closing his doors, deeply in debt and exhausted.

This might seem like a sad story all around but there's a bright silver lining. Both entrepreneurs learned something valuable about the market and they also decided that failure would not be the end of their stories. Within a few years, each become involved in more successful startups. The key they both learned, however, is to get maximum information for minimum cost. If you're going to fail, fail fast and cheap.

FIVE MAXIMUM INFORMATION STRATEGIES

If you remember nothing else at the end of this book we hope you'll remember this: *maximum information for minimum cost.* (If you're not rolling your eyes yet at how often we've mentioned this concept, we haven't hit it often enough!)

You'll likely need to examine many promising ideas before you hit on one that you might be able to leverage to create a successful new entrepreneurial venture. So the goal should be to examine and discard the bad ideas quickly in favor of the good. How do you obtain the information you need? If you don't know where else to begin, here are five near-universal strategies to pursue.

First, *conduct interviews*. Find potential customers and ask them about their challenges, their motivations and how important it is to them to solve their problems. It's much better to interview random target customers in this case, not friends or family who might shade their answers out of politeness or just to make you feel better. (If your friends shade their answers out of jealousy, then you need to make some new friends!)

Second, *ask experts*. Find people who have worked in the industry you're targeting, or who have tried similar ideas in the past. Unless you're going to be their direct competitors, you'll be surprised at how many knowledgeable people are willing to give you their time.

Third, *conduct focus groups*. These don't need to be formal events with everyone seated around a conference table and you behind a one-way mirror, although there's nothing wrong with that except for the potential expense. By asking several potential customers or others and getting them to interact with one another, you can often learn more than just by asking directly.

Fourth, *try to sell your product*, even before you've produced it. There is an ethical issue here, and possibly a legal one, so of course you don't want to take money for promises you know you won't be able to keep. But at the very least, you can gauge peoples' interest. In a best-case scenario, you might wind up with customers offering you cash before you've invested very much yourself. That's some of the best information you can possibly get.

Finally, *ask people to consider investing* in your idea. Even if you don't think you're ready to take other peoples' money yet or if you don't think you want or need to do so, people who are considering putting their money behind you are almost always going to ask hard questions. Better to force yourself to examine the answers early, before you get started.

Remember, you're looking for feedback---but more than that, you're looking for the big idea that shows you potential customers and investors are excited and will really follow through when your product or service is available for sale. It's like they say about breakfast: The chicken that provides the eggs is *interested*. The pig that provides the bacon is *committed*.

THE BIG PICTURE

We can't overemphasize how important it is that you take these core concepts to heart before you go much further: *brainstorming ideas, finding customer pain, calculating value proposition*, and *calculating market size*---all while obtaining *maximum information for minimum cost*. Getting this right helps you build the kind of solid foundation that the vast majority of entrepreneurs fail to achieve. Starting off on such stable footing makes your next steps---building and leading a great team, marshaling resources, and all the other things we'll explore the rest of the way in this book---far more likely to contribute to a fruitful new venture.

So, keep asking yourself: Where is the evidence? Where is the data? Are you offering your potential customers something valuable? Have you found the most efficient use for a resource? Is there true merit to your idea? Are you trying to be the real deal or are you just trying to get rich quickly?

It truly is a never-ending process and while it can be difficult or stressful, extraordinary entrepreneurs find great satisfaction in it. Following this framework puts powerful free market forces at your back.

If you truly believe you've hit on something useful---if it will really provide value---then you're almost morally obligated to investigate further. You can be assured that if you look hard enough, you will find that first idea---the one that you, personally, are best-equipped to make happen. It's how creative destruction works; you, the innovative outsider, are guaranteed to be the best positioned to launch *something*.

The question to keep asking yourself is, *"Is **this** my something?"*

MODULE 5

" I don't try to jump over seven-foot hurdles. I look for one-foot hurdles that I can step over. "

- Warren Buffett

COMPETITIVE ADVANTAGE, BUSINESS MODELS, & EXECUTION

When does it become time to shift from thinking about starting a new venture to actually launching it? Once you've applied the idea-generation and evaluation framework from the last three modules, you'll likely be eager to start. Before you do, however, ask yourself with a cold eye whether you've truly refined your concept to the point that your odds of success are high enough. You don't get an unlimited number of opportunities in life. Test, test, test, so that the chances you do take have a legitimate shot at winning. Smart entrepreneurs commit wholeheartedly to their ventures, but they do so only after they've reduced their risks and created great advantages for themselves.

Think back to the two general kinds of risk that entrepreneurs should consider when evaluating new ideas: business risk and technical risk. Truly great ideas include within them the seeds of strategies to mitigate both kinds of risk, but almost all ideas can benefit from risk-reducing strategies. As you get closer to committing to a new venture, focus your energy on reducing risks and creating advantages over potential competitors.

Among the hundreds of entrepreneurs we've interviewed over the years, one stands out in this department. In 1987, an experienced investor and entrepreneur named Amin Khoury set out to find an industry in which he could start a company with great competitive advantages.

"I thought about trying to find businesses where the competitive environment above all was manageable," he told us, "meaning that there weren't giant corporations with lots of capital and technology I would have to compete with ... I wanted to be in a business which would likely grow, where it might be possible for me in the future to have a market share leadership position, and where, over time, barriers to entry could evolve."

He found his answer in a niche within the aerospace industry: the companies that make equipment for airplane passenger cabins.

It turns out that airlines can't just use standard coffeemakers aboard commercial planes, for example. They are required to use FAA-certified models that won't short out and start a fire at 34,000 feet. If there is that much regulation over coffee makers, you can envision that manufacturers of more integral mechanical parts are even more heavily regulated.

Some entrepreneurs might have seen the regulatory environment as an insurmountable problem, but Khoury saw opportunity. He put together an investment group and bought what to him was small a firm---"a little business doing about $2 million in revenue"---that sold FAA-approved products. Then he set out to acquire its competitors.

Through acquisitions and organic growth, the company is now quite large. You've probably never heard of the venture Khoury created, called B/E Aerospace, unless you happen to have worked in the airline industry, but Khoury's business model includes significant competitive advantages. Government regulations, his company's size, its leverage with its customers and the fact that B/E Aerospace provides a one-stop shopping model make it very difficult for anyone else to compete with it. Let's put it this way: Want to design and sell a better airplane coffeemaker? No problem. Just submit your design and prototype for testing with the FAA, and we'll see you in the air---maybe in five to seven years.

"By combining businesses, eliminating some competition and doing some clever things in our IT department," he explained, "we were able to capture a lot of market share and grow that business well. It's a successful company, and we did a couple of billion in revenue last year."

A couple of billion dollars every year. Not bad, right? But what do you do if you don't have the opportunity or experience to get into an industry with so many ready built competitive advantages? What strategies can you use to create competitive advantages where they don't already exist and improve your new venture's prospects in the process?

CREATING COMPETITIVE ADVANTAGES

Harvard Business School Professor Michael Porter offers a useful framework to understand what positions some businesses better than others. Porter identifies five competitive forces that can threaten any business and examines how, by defending against these forces, ventures can gain enduring advantages over their competitors. Using his classic work as a guide, let's examine some of the most critical questions you should ask as you structure your thinking about business risk.

First, are there *barriers to entry* that can prevent competitors from moving into your market? That's part of what made Khoury's B/E Aerospace so attractive, of course, but other barriers might include things like significant sunk costs or brand equity that a market leader has built, or distribution channels that you or a competitor might lock up.

Second, *where competitors do exist, how intense is the competition?* Are you about to enter an industry where you'll be going head-to-head with many other players? Or have you identified something unique where you might have a bit of breathing room?

Third, how likely is it that some other product or service will *replace your industry entirely?* You want to be careful not to solve a customer pain that is about to become obsolete.

Fourth, *how much bargaining power do your customers have over you?* Are you limited to a few big customers, like Hansen Industries was when it used its wheel-alignment process to target the aerospace market? Or are you more like the guys selling Rollerblades to millions of fitness fanatics?

Finally, *how much bargaining power do your suppliers have?* Are there irreplaceable materials you absolutely have to have? Are you sure you can get them over the long term at a reasonable cost?

The more you think about these competitive forces and how they affect the venture you're considering, the better; the more you use them to create advantages that keep your potential competitors from facing off against you, the better still. Build a moat, as they say, and create an advantage for your new venture. Here are some strategies to get you started.

FORGE KEY ALLIANCES

Big players often enjoy inherent advantages that can deter an otherwise promising entrepreneur from entering a market. So why not turn that problem on its head? Find a big player who *isn't* in your particular market, team up with it and use that alliance to build an advantage. Sound too esoteric or unreasonable? It's what Robin Wolaner did when she launched *Parenting* magazine as a joint venture with Time Inc.

This can be a great strategy in almost any industry. So, don't fight the big players, necessarily; get them to join you. Imagine you want to open a local restaurant. Perhaps you could arrange to become the sole local provider of a particular brand of food people want---or else, soda, beer, wine, dessert, or something else. You see small ventures do this all the time, becoming the "authorized distributor" or "authorized partner" of a larger company--- everything from cellular telephones to automobile mechanics. With the right terms, it can be a powerful advantage.

BUILD A FINANCIAL WAR CHEST

Wouldn't this be easier if you already had a long track record or a lot of money? This isn't the whole game, of course. We could write an entire book about the hubris of the well-funded and the failures of some very well-capitalized ventures. Nevertheless, having a big bank account can indeed be a great advantage.

For example, Tesla Motors seemed on the brink of bankruptcy before it deftly convinced the U.S. government that developing an electric vehicle was important to the country for both economic and environmental reasons. The end result was that the U.S. Department of Energy guaranteed $465 million in loans so that Tesla could build a factory and produce its Model S electric car. With the government guarantee, the company went on to raise additional capital from an IPO and an investment from Toyota.

Finding investment can be difficult, but if you're armed with data about overcoming business and technical risk you can attract all sorts of investors. In today's world, there are many people and institutions seeking to invest in great new ideas. Everyone wants to fund the next Microsoft or Google. If you have a truly good idea and can convince the right people that you can execute it, sufficiently capitalizing your venture at the outset can give you a great advantage over competitors. We'll discuss how to do this in greater detail in a later module.

BUILD A POSITIVE IMAGE

If you've truly found a great solution to a genuinely felt customer pain, people might want to hear from you even before you have a chance to launch your product. As a result, it can be possible to build great word of mouth even before you start. Think about how Robin Chase created a following with Zipcar---she had the Associated Press and NPR calling her within days of putting the first green Volkswagen New Beetle on the street. Moreover, Robin Wolaner of *Parenting* had the names and contact information of thousands of people who wanted her magazine before she'd commissioned her first article.

These days, getting a story in The *Wall Street Journal* or on TechCrunch might be great, but so is the idea of a few hundred people tweeting on Twitter about you or your company. There are many books written about how to generate PR and even social media PR specifically. If you want to interest a reporter in your story or product, approach him or her as you would a customer. Ask yourself: *What is his or her pain?* Find a way to make your story the solution. Journalists need to write stories of interest to their readers---with conflict, celebrity, surprising human behavior, and politics, for example. If you can offer an opinion or insight into an ongoing public debate or controversy or else frame your story so that it relates to current news or calendar-driven events, you'll be in a much better position to get free media.

RECRUIT A GREAT TEAM

We'll spend more time later talking about recruiting the best team, but for now simply recognize that doing so can be a major competitive advantage. Look for people who actually get things done---not just those who are great at talking about concepts. Even if they're just starting in business, look at potential team members' track records (literally): What sports did they play or activities did they participate in during high school? Did they learn to be team players? Even now, what do they do outside work? If you find someone who runs marathons or competes in triathlons, you've probably found someone who is tenacious and stays motivated even when external encouragement or rewards don't come easily.

The most important consideration, however, is whether the person is a good fit for your venture. You want people with complementary skill sets and complementary styles. When a leading hotel chain wants to recruit new talent for its management-training program, for example, it pays less attention to grades and college majors than to whether applicants have been active in fraternities and sororities. Candidates are especially attractive---and might be an especially good fit---if they've served as social directors of those kinds of organizations. If you enjoy and are effective at organizing social events for college students, the thinking goes, you can probably serve customers and learn to manage a hotel.

FIRST MOVER ADVANTAGE

Many entrepreneurs primarily consider only one potential competitive advantage: first-mover advantage, which is the ability to gain customers before any competitors enter the market. In theory this is a fine strategy, but pragmatically, it can be very expensive and it can conflict with the idea of gaining maximum information for minimum cost. Think about first-mover advantage as just that: an advantage. It's not a complete game plan, and the first entrepreneur to enter a market with a new product doesn't always survive.

We've already talked about one recent example: online social networks. The current leader in the United States is Facebook, but Facebook followed in the footsteps of many previous entrants. A partial list might include theGlobe.com, SixDegrees.com, AOL, Friendster, MySpace, and others.

There are many other ways you can create competitive advantage. You can focus on creating an enhanced user experience. You can leverage or build social proof---everything from "buzz" that you might be able to create on online social networks to reaching out and getting the kind of great blurbs and accolades that might have enticed you to buy this book. The bottom line is that creating competitive advantage is an integral part of the entrepreneurial process. If you don't think you can beat the competitors at their own game, find a way to change the rules, and goad them into playing *your* game instead.

BUSINESS EXAMPLE: A NON-FIRST MOVER'S COMPETITIVE ADVANTAGE

Who is your mobile phone provider today? Verizon? AT&T? Practically none of today's industry leaders existed in its current form at the inception of this market. The first movers that dominated the field and scared away other competitors back in the 1980s have since consolidated, been driven out of the industry, or even folded.

The first U.S. cellular phone company to do business with the general public was Ameritech, one of the offspring of the Bell System breakup, in 1983. It dominated its market---but its operations were limited to one metropolitan area, Chicago, because of the way the U.S. Federal Communications Commission allocated frequencies for mobile phones at the time. Ameritech and similar companies had a seven-year head start before an entrepreneur named Craig McCaw bought up regional licenses in many cities, and linked them together to launch Cellular One---the first truly nationwide roaming network.

The cell phone story goes one step further. McCaw sold the CellularOne network to AT&T, and then in 1994, he did the whole thing again. By buying frequencies that the FCC had originally allocated for a sort of cellular walkie-talkie service, and by piggybacking traditional mobile telephone service onto it, his new company, Nextel, built a national cellular network almost literally overnight. This was a major coup, built with an inherent competitive advantage over Nextel's rivals. Not only did Nextel have a second national network, but regulations would also make it difficult for any other rivals to replicate what he'd done.

You might think an entrepreneur would be crazy to try to launch a new cellular phone network to compete with all the entrenched market leaders, but the history of the industry in America is that new entrants, not the first mover, have in fact won, time and again. All things being equal, is it better to be first? Maybe, but things are rarely equal. Other advantages can often rule the day.

REDUCING TECHNICAL RISK

Remember that when we discussed calculating a value proposition, we argued that one reason for doing so is that it can focus your attention on the attributes of your model that need improvement. As we deduced the production costs in calculating the value proposition of a grande soy latte, for example, we inherently examined the technical risks involved in producing them. Taking this calculation apart and figuring out ways to reduce that technical risk can lead to formidable competitive advantages in any business.

Sometimes measuring technical risk is fairly easy. If your hope is to start a straightforward retail website, for example, all you have to do is look at some of the tens of thousands of others doing exactly the same thing in different fields and emulate their best practices.

For other new ventures, though, technical risk is a bigger deal. If you're pursuing an idea that requires newer or less common technology, it helps to break things into stages---*lab*, *prototype*, and *full scale production*---and consider at each point how promising your business remains. Let's see what this entails.

There are two natural tendencies that you need to be aware of, whether you're going to be using a highly technical manufacturing process or starting a more people-centered business in which you provide services to a customer. One of these tendencies, *increasing efficiency*, generally works in your favor as you scale. The other, *decreasing yield*, can easily work against you if you are not careful.

You hope to gain efficiency as you scale up, but also maintain or even improve quality of your product. Unfortunately, you're far more likely to see your quality decrease, even if on the surface you seem to be producing products or providing services more efficiently.

Let's use a simple example. Suppose you're launching a consulting business or a professional services business like a law office or an accounting firm. Your efficiency should go up as you take on new clients. You don't need to create a new billing system for every new client, for example, and you might be able to recycle at least part of the work you do for one client when you do work for another. On the other hand, there are only so many hours in the day, so quality can suffer. If you divide your time among three clients, each gets more attention and perhaps better care than if you divide your time among 10, 20, or even 50 clients.

This observation illuminates the relative attractiveness of some different business ideas. In essence, there are only two ways for a person to make money. You can rent or sell assets, including *money* itself. (The insightful reader will note that one way to make a lot of money is to rent or sell other people's money---in the form of either equity or debt.) Or else, you can rent or sell your *time*---whether it means working for a full-time employer, or launching a business where you offer your services by the hour. Of course, when you sell your time, you're limited by the fact that there are only 168 hours in a week.

Books have been written and careers have been made on promoting efficiency and maintaining quality as firms scale. We especially recommend reading the work of W. Edwards Deming and Peter F. Drucker. Large organizations have come a long way in adopting structural quality management, using disciplines such as ISO 9000, QS 9000, and the Six Sigma management strategy. When starting a business, you're naturally going to focus on improving your products and services. Implementing large-scale quality management programs might seem like overkill. Still, it's worth taking a page from the bigger players' books, and building structures to ensure that you maintain and improve the quality of your offerings as you grow larger.

TESTING AND MEASURING TECHNICAL RISK

If you want to envision quickly what technical risk and quality control are all about, think of the scene from the old TV series *I Love Lucy* in which Lucy and her friend Ethel get jobs on an assembly line in a candy factory. Unable to keep up with the pace of the line, they start pulling the candies off the conveyor belt, eating them, and stuffing them into their clothing.

Remember Lucy when you think about scaling your business. People make mistakes. Processes break down. Inevitably, there will be "lemons." Your *yield*---the percentage of products that survive the production process with sufficient quality to meet standards---will suffer as you scale.

In the semiconductor industry, for example, it's common to endure low production yields in early chip fabrication runs. If you're a lawyer, your eyes will get groggy and you'll probably miss a comma in a legal document every now and again. If you open a cupcake bakery, once in a while you'll burn a batch.

So, what do we do about this? For one thing, you might want to think through the procedures and quality assurance methods you'll use ahead of time, even in the early stages of a new venture. This could run the gamut from implementing a formal quality assurance strategy to simply coming up with checklists so that you don't forget things in the excitement of perfecting your product or dealing with customers.

As always, you want to get the maximum information you can about the pitfalls you'll likely face ahead of time, for minimum cost. Attacking this problem requires interviewing others in the industry and doing research before you begin. Again, research, research, research. You can find a range of private or published yield rates for just about any industry. The earlier in the process you can predict your potential yield, the better.

Customer Acquisition Cost

If you want to reduce business risk (and thus create advantages), here's an important question that many entrepreneurs fail to examine sufficiently: *What will it cost to acquire each new customer?* At any point, whether you're just considering launching a business or else years into your operation, you'd ideally like to be able to make this calculation quickly.

Neglecting customer acquisition cost is an understandable and common mistake. If you've built your business ideas around solving customers' real pain, you might assume that customers will flock to you. The problem is that there are always costs expended in getting new customers, and they're often much greater than you anticipate.

In general, we can break the customer acquisition process down into three steps: First, as an entrepreneur, you need to identify customer *leads*. Second, you need to qualify those leads, to see if you can turn them into *prospects*. Finally, you want to move in for the sale, and turn prospects into *customers*.

Here's an example. Say you wanted to calculate the customer acquisition cost for a business like Zipcar. You'd start by generating customer leads, which basically means anyone you have reason to believe may have some interest in your product or service. That's a pretty low barrier, but it's a barrier nonetheless. For example, in its earliest days, Zipcar might have pursued any one of a number of strategies to identify leads. The company might have sent direct mail or Internet solicitations to every person over the age of 18 living in Cambridge, Massachusetts or within five blocks of one of its cars. Perhaps they went to community and civic events and handed out flyers. Robin Chase and her crew might have had no idea whether the people they reached owned cars, or liked driving, or were dissatisfied with their transportation options---but they could at least be sure they were more likely to become customers than, say, a bunch of 15-year-old boys living in another city entirely. A lead can be anyone---someone you've actively gone out and found or even someone who happens just to walk into the door of your retail store to get out of the rain.

The next step, then, is to *qualify the lead*, so that you can move it into the category of *prospect*. In the case of Zipcar, Chase would have wanted to figure out things like whether her leads had driver's licenses, whether they had enough money to become customers, whether they had good credit, and whether they had so many speeding tickets that they'd be impossible to insure.

The rate of conversion from leads to prospects will vary wildly depending on your business, and you can see how important it is to calculate market size ahead of time. After you launch is no time to realize that there are a lot of people who might find your product interesting or cool, but for whom there are insurmountable barriers that will prevent you from ever qualifying them as customer prospects.

Now, finally, we reach the stage where many entrepreneurs think we actually begin: the point where you work your magic and try to turn the *prospect* into a *customer*. This is when you get to convince your potential customer to try the value proposition on for size, and hopefully pay you for what you have to offer.

At each step in the process, only a fraction of leads or prospects advances on. Figuring out what that percentage is or could consistently be over time, along with the overall cost of identifying leads or prospects to begin with, allows us to figure out the average *customer acquisition cost*. That's a very important number to know. It can provide an early warning sign about the health of your business model if it isn't satisfactory. Identifying things that make it easier or harder to convert customers can also reduce your business risk and help you create advantages over competitors.

So, what would Zipcar's customer acquisition cost be in this example?

It's really a matter of simple math. Add up the cost of all the measures required to identify leads, qualify them as prospects, and convert them to customers---and then divide that number by the number of customers. Suppose Zipcar had $10,000 to spend on marketing pieces in the first few days and that it cost another $10,000 in employee time and effort to qualify leads and convince its first 500 customers to join. In that case, the customer acquisition cost would be $40 each ($20,000 divided by 500).

LIFETIME VALUE OF A CUSTOMER

Before we can complete this discussion of reducing business risk, we need to examine another critical calculation: *the lifetime value of a customer.* How much profit will a customer generate for your firm during a given time period, adjusted by the inevitable percentage of customers you can expect to lose over the same period?

Think about how the structure of some businesses can inherently affect these values. For example, suppose your dream is to open a bed and breakfast in the hills of Vermont or the wine country of Northern California. If so, the lifetime value of your customers probably isn't all that high. It's great that people love staying with you, but most Americans only take a few weeks of vacation per year. They don't always return to the same region.

Imagine, instead, that you were to launch an online subscription service, like a dating website. The lifetime value of your customers would likely be higher, as you renew your customers' memberships every month. In fact, one of the biggest limitations you might find on generating perpetual revenue is if the dating site becomes too successful, and too many customers wind up in long-term relationships.

Let's think about this in the context of Zipcar again. If our sample $40 per customer acquisition cost was accurate, determining whether that was a good deal or not would depend greatly on the lifetime value of each customer. Let's assume that after signing up for the service each customer generated an average of $500 in profit for Zipcar over the duration of their relationship with the company. (To be even more accurate here, you would want to calculate the net present value of the future profits.) In this simplified example, each new customer represents a lifetime value to Zipcar of $460. That's certainly a compelling business.

So, apply this to your business idea. How often do you project your customers will return to buy from you again? How does that compare to the customer acquisition cost? Are there things you can do to increase the lifetime value, or else reduce the cost required to acquire each customer?

These are great little bits of data to have before you launch full-force into business, and yet it probably won't surprise you that most entrepreneurs don't do the math ahead of time. Armed with these kinds of simple calculations, you'll be in much better shape than many competitors.

BUSINESS EXAMPLE: BUILDING ADVANTAGES INTO A BUSINESS MODEL

Have you ever wasted hours trying to set up a computer, printer, or network just so that you can ultimately *begin* to do the things you truly needed to

get done? At a large company, the solution might
be to call the IT department, but if you're running
a smaller business, you probably are your own IT
department.

In 1998, an entrepreneur named Tim Mott
who had already helped create Electronic Arts and
Macromedia---in other words a guy who had run a
few businesses in his time---took notice of this fact
and built a business around it. The result was All
Covered, a company specializing in outsourced IT
support for small and medium businesses.

"It was an opportunity that was being neglected
and overlooked," Mott told us in an interview. "A
lot of people don't understand the size of the small
business segment in the economy, and I was shocked.
To me this was [previously] all about enterprises like
IBM, Bank of America, and American Express."

Firms with fewer than a hundred people, Mott
noted, account for half of America's gross domestic
product. They often had no infrastructure at all in
place to take care of their IT needs. Rather than
providing an on-call service that would rush out to
handle small companies' computer problems on a
one-time basis, however, All Covered was established

as a subscription service. Companies would pay a monthly fee based on the number of users and computers in the business, and they would be entitled to a certain number of service hours per month.

It's a great business model for at least three reasons.

First, All Covered generally only signs its clients once, so customer acquisition costs are comparatively low. Second, most customers won't actually need much IT support; their monthly payment is as much for the security of knowing that they will be able to handle IT problems easily if they every do come up. Finally---and this goes back to creating competitive advantage---Mott's company didn't set out to become the leading outsourced IT company. Instead, it redefined the playing field, and set out to become the leading outsourced IT provider in a new, segmented market.

The best kind of customer can be the customer you already have. All Covered has worked hard to find the Holy Grail of most business models: *recurring revenue*---a customer who costs you nothing or almost nothing to retain but keeps buying your products over and over again.

SELECTING A BUSINESS MODEL

Start thinking about how you can acquire customers and get them to purchase your products over and over again, and you run into a basic structural question: What is your business model? By business model, we mean the ongoing process of producing, offering, selling, and collecting payment for the value proposition you've put together. How do you organize your inputs, processes, and delivery to your customers? To put it a bit more metaphorically, how do you build the merry-go-round and get it going so that it comes closest to approaching a perpetual motion machine---one that solves problems, improves the world, and regularly wires payments to your savings and checking accounts?

Let's start with what Bill Sahlman, professor of entrepreneurship at Harvard Business School, calls the ideal business model: a post office box where people endlessly send you cashier's checks. (Please, sign us up!) Setting aside for the moment the question of whether such a "business" would improve the world in some way, there's a lot of tremendously useful guidance in Sahlman's model. Imagine if you could build a business in which, for whatever reason, people simply sent you money. What kinds of characteristics would it have?

Well, it would require low levels of customer contact. That's a good thing, all else being equal, because customer contact costs money. Next, it would have low capital requirements---little more than the cost of the mailbox. It would have minimal logistical requirements. Stop by the mailbox once or twice a week, maybe swing by the bank, and you'd be all set. Moreover, you'd have timely payments, huge profit margins, and virtually no risk.

Simple, and lucrative! It's hard to imagine any real-life business model that would live up to that model, of course, but if you use Sahlman's thought experiment as your ideal and measure whatever you come up with against it, it suddenly becomes a lot easier to gauge the desirability of various business models. Let's give it a try.

Suppose you're Elon Musk, and you want to launch a space transport company: SpaceX. Measure the business model of SpaceX against the Sahlman ideal and it's a potentially tough venture. Customer contact costs are high. Can you imagine the sales and service effort to convince someone to pay to launch satellites into orbit? Capital requirements and risk are huge: just mention that it's a spaceship company and you're suddenly talking about many hundreds of millions of dollars. Logistical requirements are similarly high, and payments and profit margins are largely unknown.

Thank goodness that there are people willing and able to take considered risks like this to achieve noteworthy goals. These kinds of high-risk, high-reward businesses are crucial to societal advancement, and perhaps the purest examples of creative destruction in action. That said, entrepreneurs need to walk before they run. If you're reading this book as a guide to entrepreneurship and starting your own company, you're probably *not* yet an Elon Musk, who has already launched a number of very successful companies already.

Let's consider a few more common differentiated business models. As we go through these, consider how well they stack up against the Sahlman post office box ideal.

RAZORS AND RAZOR BLADES

This is such a classic and effective business model that we refer to it simply by the name of the product that perfected it first. Razors are generally sold at or below cost. Razor *blades*, on the other hand---that's where they get you. You can see how the model has been applied to other industries, too. Today, for example, you can buy a decent laser printer for $50 on sale, but it will cost you $60 or $70 for a replacement toner cartridge. For that matter, John Osher of Spinbrush did this with his mid-range electric toothbrushes, because he sold replacement heads and other parts for them.

SUBSCRIPTION PUBLISHING

The traditional form of this model has taken a beating, witnessed by the challenges befalling many of the world's newspaper and magazine publishers. Electronic content and advertising present a formidable challenge. Even so, entrepreneurs from Arianna Huffington to Rupert Murdoch have been trying to implement new business models to transition the industry. People write stories, advertisers place ads, material is published either in print or electronically, and the reader pays for the content---by subscribing to a newspaper or magazine, for example, or by paying the monthly cable or satellite television bill. The Internet has introduced a great deal of tumult in the publishing world. Physical magazines and newspapers shrink, while online resources mushroom. No one yet knows the steady-state business model, but there sure are a lot of entrepreneurs trying to figure it out.

LOW-COST PROVIDER

If the product or service you're offering is a commodity, perhaps you can simply undercut your competition at every turn. This business model typically requires significant economies of scale---becoming either the biggest provider in the industry, or obtaining the cheapest inputs. Think of some of the successful companies that have pulled this off: Southwest Airlines and RyanAir, for example, IKEA in furniture and Old Navy in low-cost fashions. For that matter, what about overseas call-centers, or more recently, overseas providers of more technical work? As professionals like engineers and lawyers approach commodity status, low-cost providers in other countries can make this business model work for Western clients.

PRESTIGE BRANDS

It's tricky, but if you can promise and deliver a combination of exclusivity, fashion or passion---or otherwise just satisfy customers' psychological needs to have the latest and greatest, you can build a winner. Marketing budgets are typically large, though consumer tastes are fickle. Keep in mind that in these businesses, you're likely solving intangible customer pain---things like desire for status and self-worth.

DISTRIBUTOR/CONSOLIDATOR

This business model never goes out of style. Today, you can go on Amazon or to Costco and buy fashionable clothing, a riding mower, and even a new car. How different is that model from the early US department stores, like Macy's in New York City back in the 1930s or Sears Roebuck & Co. even before that? One hundred years ago, you could even order blueprints and materials to build a prefabricated house from Sears. Maybe you don't need to be the best provider of any one product or service, if you can offer convenience and one-stop shopping.

SPECIALTY PROVIDER

This is the opposite of the distributor/consolidator model. Here, you pick one thing and do it better than anyone else. Today, high-end department stores might sell all of the top clothing and makeup brands, and yet independent, one-label clothing stores and specialty apothecaries are thriving. This can work in professional services as well. Imagine that you were to start a law firm that specialized in same-sex family law, or modern U.S. veterans' benefits. You might find it easier to convince clients that you were better and worth more money than a more general provider.

MARKET MAKER

Difficult and ambitious as this can be, suppose you could start a specialty auction house or site or else even a stock exchange. This is the eBay model, but it's also the model used by things like Cars. com, and the entire residential real estate industry. By creating a marketplace, you develop opportunities for other entrepreneurs--- and then usually take a percentage of every transaction. It can be very lucrative.

USER-PRODUCED CONTENT

Generally, the more user-produced your product is, the better. Some online models probably spring quickly to mind---YouTube, for example, as well as LinkedIn or Facebook, in which the users themselves produce virtually all of the content. But these products exist in the non-virtual world as well. When a customer pumps her own gas or checks out his groceries at a self-service cash register, there's the potential to reduce the cost of servicing each customer. When a restaurant shifts to a take-out model (as opposed to sit-down or delivery service), but charges the same prices on the menu, that can make a lot of sense from a business model perspective.

Monopoly/Oligarchy

When we talk about monopolies, we're talking primarily about companies in industries with such great barriers to entry that competitors simply can't get a toehold. Perhaps the startup costs are just so high that few competitors will be in a position to try. Perhaps the first-mover's advantage will have sustained to such a degree that new entrants will be at a real disadvantage. Perhaps patents, professional licenses, or other government regulations are enough to keep competitors out.

Only one American industry is explicitly allowed to control a near-total monopoly: professional baseball. No joke; an old U.S. Supreme Court decision that has never been overturned found that baseball was an "amusement," as opposed to a "commercial enterprise" and that it was therefore exempt from antitrust law.

That said, many other companies that have successfully created monopolistic or near-monopolistic status for themselves over the years. At least until the government antitrust authorities get involved, it's a heck of a model: the Bell System, for example, in the 1970s and 1980s, Microsoft, in the late 1990s, and quite conceivably, Amazon or Google in the 2010s.

THE BIG PICTURE

To revisit the question we asked at the start of this module, how do you know when it's time to transition from thinking about launching to doing so? The answer is probably when you can confidently answer "yes" to several important questions. Have you identified an acute customer pain and offered a compelling solution? Have you calculated an attractive value proposition? Is there a large enough market so as to be worth your time and effort? Continue to ask yourself if you've identified the best possible business model. Have you figured out great strategies to reduce your technical and business risk, and identified ways to create competitive advantage?

It's often difficult to pinpoint the exact moment, but there is a time when the process of refining the idea becomes the process of actually starting a business. You'll realize that you need to attract the best possible designers, engineers, or salespeople; you'll decide that perhaps you need to raise more money; you'll determine that you need to align yourself with the biggest players in your industry---and you'll simply decide to do it.

And yet, you might reasonably ask at this point---how do I get these things when I haven't actually started yet? Don't I have a classic chicken-and-egg problem? How do I convince the people who will help me achieve these competitive advantages to join before I've even begun?

In other words how do you become credible as an entrepreneur before you've actually achieved all the things you hope you will achieve? That's exactly what we'll be examining in the next module.

MODULE 6

"You can't build a reputation on what you are going t do."

-Henry Ford

BUILDING CREDIBILITY

Why should anyone else believe you can do this?

For some readers, until now it might seem as if, until now, this has been a book about how *other people* become successful entrepreneurs, as opposed to how *you* can do it. How do you make yourself *feel* like an entrepreneur before you become one? How do you train yourself to embrace the attitude of entrepreneurial inevitability? It's one thing to read a book or watch a video on how tango; it's another entirely to get out there and dance.

Taking that a step further, how do you convince the rest of the world that you're now an entrepreneur? Not just a dreamer, or a big talker, but someone who will accomplish important things.

The point of this module is to help you take the first steps across that bridge. There are strategies you can employ ahead of time to legitimately increase your credibility and, in the process, improve your plan.

In the course of writing this book, we had the chance to quite literally follow one successful serial founder as he demonstrated how it's done.

John Scharffenberger is a bona fide specialty food expert, with an impressive track record of taking foods that are popular in Europe or elsewhere in the world and making them popular in America. He began his entrepreneurial journey as a winemaker, growing grapes and making a California sparkling wine that looked and tasted like fine French champagne. Then, after he built and sold Scharffenberger Cellars, he got into the high-end chocolate business. Over the course of a decade, Scharffenberger and his business partner Robert Steinberg built Scharffen Berger Chocolate, then sold it to Hershey for $50 million.

We caught up with Scharffenberger and walked with him through Berkeley, California on a beautiful summer day as he was about to enter yet another new business. He'd been considering a book and a documentary TV series about the history of chocolate, he explained, but the idea that really excited him was a new company that would specialize in---of all things---gourmet tofu.

As Scharffenberger walked, he kept reaching into a big plastic bag he carried, offering the contents---tofu samples---to people he met along the way: *Do you like tofu?* he called out. *You're going to love this tofu. Just wait until you try this tofu!*

He stopped for lunch at a trendy place called Restaurant 900 Grayson, where he offered a piece of tofu to the chef and approached other acquaintances, enthusiastically saying hello, then, *You have to try this tofu! This is the most amazing tofu!*

Truth to tell, we're not sure if anyone really likes tofu. But Berkeley has a foodie reputation, and Scharffenberger is well known in the Bay Area for his palate, and his deep passion for fine foods. If John Scharffenberger was so excited about a piece of tofu, people seemed to think, it might be worth trying.

But Scharffenberger already has credibility, right? Before tofu, he had chocolate. Before chocolate, he had wine. But what did he have before that?

What did he do to build credibility when he was an unknown 22-year-old with a good idea and almost no money or track record? What can his experience teach you?

Establishing Credibility

When you were a kid, maybe your mom told you something along the lines of, "Don't worry about what anyone else thinks!" We're sure your mother was a wonderful woman, but there's a reason she probably wasn't a hugely successful entrepreneur. (If you're Alexis Stewart, Martha's daughter, save your receipt and contact us for a full refund of the purchase price of this book.)

An entrepreneur's entire reason for being is to solve customers' pain, but customers won't buy from you unless they believe in you first. What's more, unless you at least appear to be on track to gain customers, other would-be stakeholders won't help you. You need to recruit great team members who will both help you build and sell your product, and help you build credibility with customers. You might need to raise capital so that you can recruit those great people, acquire assets, and, once again attract customers.

Starting to notice a theme yet? Eventually, it always comes back to customers.

If your venture's promise is truly compelling, customers will probably *want* to believe in it. But, we've all seen too many infomercials and too many salespeople who promise more than they can back up.

Credibility is therefore crucial, and there are two recurring elements to building it.

First, and this should be no surprise, *focus on the customer.* In fact, this is good advice for every aspect of the entrepreneurial process. When you have days or moments when you're not sure what you should be doing, stop and ask yourself: What can I do right now that does the most to relieve my customers' pain?

Second, *start with small steps and build on them.* Success begets success, so set short-term goals, achieve milestones, and celebrate them (but don't rest on your laurels). For example, many entrepreneurs will write a regular, short newsletter for family, friends, and stakeholders, telling them what they plan to do in the coming week or month. Then, they'll hold themselves accountable in the next missive, celebrating those achievements when they meet or surpass them while setting out even loftier goals. (If you want to see a company newsletter that worked out pretty well, check out of the archives at http://www.google.com/googlefriends/archive.html.)

The more small victories you can amass, the better you'll feel. More importantly, the more credible you'll be when it comes to trying to convince the next potential stakeholder that you're the real deal. Small "wins" create a powerful momentum. The snowball effect works.

Let's look back at how John Scharffenberger did this in order to build credibility each time he entered a new industry. Before he got into sparkling wine, he explained to us, he took very small steps. He traveled to the Champagne region of France, where he fixed tractors and studied the business. He started out with very little capital, so when he applied for loans he started small, targeting banks that had previously loaned money to the vineyards whose grapes he'd need to make his wine. (By lending him money, those banks would be helping their other borrowers, too.) He had almost no advertising budget compared to his competitors, so again he started small. He threw parties at San Francisco bars, invited Bay Area food industry workers, and gave them bottles of his champagne.

He cultivated his reputation as carefully as he cultivated his grapes, courting tastemakers and developing an encyclopedic knowledge. Each success built his credibility, and was in turn built on a previous, smaller success. Even after he'd launched and sold two companies---the winery and the chocolate company---Scharffenberger employed the same kind of strategy when he wanted to enter yet another new business. That's what he was doing when he walked around with a shopping bag full of gourmet tofu and handed it out to people. He was testing the market, but more importantly, sharing his small successes step by small step, literally to one person at a time--- *finding this great new tofu!*---and further building his credibility.

STRATEGIES FOR ESTABLISHING CREDIBILITY

In his book, *Influence: The Psychology of Persuasion*, author Robert Cialdini describes six methods people can use to persuade others of just about anything: *reciprocity, consistency, social proof, authority, likability, and scarcity*. It's worth considering Cialdini's framework as we examine how entrepreneurs can bolster credibility.

Let's take ***reciprocity*** first. People are more likely to offer to do something if they feel like they're returning a small favor or repaying a debt. So, as an entrepreneur, be the one who offers to help people even when there's no obvious or guaranteed way they'll be able to help you in return. Offer small giveaways to potential customers to get their attention. Make it easy for customers to try you out with no outlay or commitment, and they just might factor the gratitude into the decision to become a real customer.

Second, be *consistent.* People respect others who honor their commitments. So, arrive on time. Meet your milestones. Think back to how Robin Chase practically tore her hair out in order to meet the launch date she'd promised the city of Cambridge. The date itself didn't truly mean much, but the fact that she followed through mattered a lot. Come through on small promises, and you'll be in a better position when you start asking customers for larger commitments.

Next, you want to find ways to obtain *social proof.* The more people who use your product or service---and who are likely to talk about it---the better. Think about some of the ways the entrepreneurs we've examined focused on this. Every customer of Zipcar became an advertiser, with the big "Z" logo on the side of the cars. PayPal users had to advertise their use of the product in order to make it worthwhile---otherwise the people they wanted to send or receive money from wouldn't know where to go. It was only after Jim Koch won a contest that declared Samuel Adams Boston Lager the best-tasting beer in America that the brand gained some momentum. Make it easy for customers to choose you by showing them that other people choose you, too.

Much as customers look to peers for advice on what products and services to buy, they also look to *authority.* They want to know that the pain relievers they use are the ones that top athletes use after games, that the government says the cars they drive are the safest available, and that "four out of five dentists" think it's a good idea to chew their brand of gum. Maybe we don't like to think that we reflexively heed authority, but the truth is people do so more often than they admit. So try to become the expert or authority in your field. If you can't do that immediately, borrow authority by recruiting other figures to endorse your product. In the words of the great philosopher John Mellencamp, "Authority always wins."

Next up: *likability*. There's a reason why the hostess at a restaurant is almost always a cute young woman. There's a reason why the car salesman comes running up with a smile and insists on calling you by name. There's a reason why Google spread its corporate motto (*don't be evil*) far and wide. The more that people personally like or are attracted to a persuader, the more likely they are to comply with a request. So be genuine and likeable. A true entrepreneur believes he or she is honored to help customers solve their pain.

Finally, there's the notion of *scarcity*. People want what they can't have. Additionally, people are often indecisive. You can force their hands a bit by demonstrating that if they don't move now, they might lose out forever. So you can offer products or services for a limited time only. You can limit the number of products sold, or else consider raising prices instead of discounting.

FUNDAMENTALS OF CREDIBILITY

It's the classic chicken and egg dilemma: You need to show results in order to convince stakeholders to believe in you, but you need the help of many of those same would-be stakeholders in order to achieve results.   Getting that merry-go-round going requires building credibility before you even get started.

These days, anyone can at least *look* like he or she is starting a company, with a website, a few hundred embossed business cards, a semi-custom logo, and a voicemail service that can make a microscopic venture sound more like Microsoft.   But that's a problem, isn't it? When it's easy for just about anyone to gather the trappings of a legitimate company, the trappings don't mean very much.

So, how can you persuade people that you're more Amazon than Yugo?   There are four broad types of credibility for an entrepreneur. Assess candidly how credible you are in each category, and you can figure out what needs shoring up.

PERSONAL CREDIBILITY

When you visit a company's website, there's always a page or two describing the previous accomplishments of its founders. Why?   Because a startup's credibility is derived from the personal reputations of the organization's leaders.   So, ask yourself: *Would I buy a product or service from me?*   How compelling is the value proposition you've put together?   Can you explain how the insights you came up with led you to it?   This is also one of the reasons it is so important to enter an industry or market where you might know something ahead of time.   Remember, you don't need to be the most knowledgeable person, but you need to know *something*, and you need to be able to learn quickly.

TEAM CREDIBILITY

One-person entrepreneurial success stories are as rare as steak tartar, so you're almost always going to be recruiting teams of founders, leaders, and key contributors. How well this team covers all the bases and works together is an important part of the credibility of the whole venture. Is your team comprised purely of technical experts? Or are they a healthy, cohesive, and talented combination of product specialists, business veterans, and other needed players? How well do they fit with each other in terms of personality and personal experience? Have the founders and other key leaders worked together with each other successfully before? Or are they newcomers who might devolve into an unproductive rivalry?

ORGANIZATIONAL CREDIBILITY

Stepping beyond the founders and key employees, consider everyone and everything else who affects the success of the venture. Who do you choose to work with, and who is willing to work with you? Are the professional service people you've hired the kind of people who lend credence to your venture? Has your lawyer helped founders start other successful companies? Is your accountant trustworthy? Or will potential stakeholders recognize your lawyer from a big advertisement on the side of a city bus and your accountant from old news stories about Bernie Madoff? Moreover, where are you geographically? A new technology venture's Silicon Valley address might offer it a bit of credibility, and a financial services company located in New York City might have an advantage over one located farther from the financial hub of the Western world. Want to export lobsters all over the U.S.? The right kind of ZIP code (say, 04101, in Portland, Maine) might help.

CREDIBILITY OF PRODUCTS, SERVICES & INDUSTRY

The fundamentals that we've talked about in previous modules matter: Customer pain. Value proposition. Business and technical risk. Market size. But another aspect of credibility has to do with how well you can explain each of these factors. For example, while it's important that your venture addresses a compelling customer pain, it's also important that you can effectively *describe* how you solve it. Remember the test we used for whether a business addresses an acute customer pain: Can you explain in a single sentence what your business does and why? Potential customers need to know, as do potential employees and investors.

Related to this is the question of whether the industry you're entering makes sense on its own merits. You might have built a fantastic team, be advised by top-notch people, and developed an innovative way to solve a customer need in your market. But if your market just isn't booming, and especially if you appear to be charging forth heedlessly, your credibility can be undercut. Planning to get into the mortgage industry today, with record low interest rates and projected low inflation? Want to enter the electric car field, when the big players already need the U.S. government to guarantee their loans and Americans haven't yet bought many of the cars without big tax breaks? How do you think making those kinds of strategic business decisions would affect your credibility?

Communicating Credibility

In business, laryngitis is lethal. If you're confident about how well you stack up against the four types of credibility, then you'll normally want to sing and scream to attract would-be stakeholders' attention. (Again, don't forget that your number one category of would-be stakeholders consists of your customers.) Very often, though, entrepreneurs can't find their voices. Either they can't effectively communicate how great their products and services are or, what's worse, they hamper their efforts by unwittingly sending inaccurate messages that suggest they're illegitimate. Let's look at a few areas to increase your credibility:

Online presence

What's the first thing most people will do when they hear about your business? They'll look you up on Google. Your Internet identity is therefore crucial and you need to monitor how you and your venture are portrayed on blogs, Wikipedia, and the like. Are you on the first page of Google results---not just in searches for your name and your venture's name, but also your industry or market? If not, you need to fix that, and that means researching search engine optimization (SEO) and tailoring your marketing to maximize search results. Also, what will people find when they look for you personally? Will the results make them trust you more or less? Of course, this could mean different things for different people and ventures. If the first five entries for your name on Google are photos from a college toga party straight out of *Animal House*, this could be a problem---unless you're going into the business of planning big parties (or maybe selling togas). As an entrepreneur, you're trying to become a public figure in certain circles, so think about the messages you'll be sending with the information you post on Facebook, LinkedIn, Twitter, and the like.

Register your venture's domain name early and grab all of the similar email addresses and usernames you can on popular websites. For example, if you're writing a book called *Breakthrough Entrepreneurship*, then you probably want to grab breakthroughentrepreneurship.com, breakthroughentrepreneurship@gmail.com, @breakthroughE on Twitter, breakthroughentrepreneurship.tumblr.com, and so on. This is just a $10 investment, but nothing says fly-by-night like a domain whose *whois* information shows it was only registered a few days ago.

PRESS HITS

We truly hope that *Wired* and *Fast Company* will line up to interview you, and that your email inbox will suddenly be filled with queries from reporters at *The Wall Street Journal* and blogs like TechCrunch. However, you typically need to garner other media hits before the larger outlets will cover you.

So what do you do if you're having trouble getting anyone in the media to pay attention? Likeability and attractiveness can help, as well as reciprocity. Stop thinking of news organizations as your target, and instead think of the people who work at those organizations as individuals. Build rapport with reporters by letting them know you've taken the time to become familiar with their work---and do it before your competitors do. Journalists are human, and you're likely to get farther with a bit of respect and genuine compliments.

Give them pitches about how your product or service works in a particular region, or for a particular industry that they cover, for example. Another strategy can be to pitch stories in which your venture isn't the main hook, but in which it is portrayed as an important (and positively portrayed) supporting actor. Provide a quote for articles about larger trends. This will mean an opportunity for the reporter to at least mention your new company briefly, and will help build the foundation of your credibility in the press.

You need to find hooks or "news pegs." For example, if you're running a cupcake bakery, you might look at the calendar and figure out what holidays or other dates offer the chance to talk about your product. Maybe you'll build a float out of cupcakes for the local Fourth of July parade, or convince a reporter to write about silly "national days," like National Cupcake Day. (Yes, really. It's December 15.)

Establishing legitimate personal connections can go a long way, too. Maybe you and the reporter have some personal characteristic in common---fellow native Philadelphians, sisters in Delta Sigma Theta, or long-suffering fans of the NHL's Toronto Maple Leafs. Or maybe you can say---truthfully, of course, this is you're credibility we're talking about---that you're a fan of the reporter's writing. You might step back and try to find connections with other people at the same organization and then ask that person to forward your message along to a specific writer. That isn't always enough to get someone to write about you, but it might be enough to get him or her to listen.

AWARDS, WHITE PAPERS & OTHER MEDIA

There are likely many awards out there that your new company might qualify for, but you can't win if you don't apply. If you are truly addressing an important customer pain, you'll likely be victorious in at least some of them. The more you gain accolades, the more you garner social proof and authority status.

Whether you find a contest for product design or innovation, or for things like customer service and satisfaction, being mentioned and recognized like this can build credibility. It even becomes self-reinforcing; if you win one award, you're more likely to win the next one. (If you get stuck, try contacting us, and see if we name you to the *Top 100 Businesses Founded by Readers of Breakthrough Entrepreneurship*.)

There are business plan competitions that you can enter before you even launch---and just imagine how it might help you win credibility with investors to say you were a finalist in a business plan competition associated with a university or a chamber of commerce, for example. Moreover, these contests often come with cash prizes. In the early days of your venture, that might be just as important.

In a different vein, think about writing white papers or other "state of the art" or "state of the industry" articles. Suppose you were starting a bedbug extermination company, for example. Which sounds more credible: the company with the flashy website, or the more ambitious one with the website that links to the 172-page treatise its co-founders published entitled, *A Guide to the Environmentally Responsible Eradication of Cimex Lectularius?*

Finally, think about writing op-ed pieces, trend articles for trade magazines, or guest blog posts. Offer articles to news aggregation sites like The Huffington Post, Newser, The Daily Beast, and specialty blogs in the industry you're entering. There is an insatiable demand for media content and innumerable channels through which you can spread the word. Make yourself the Scharffenberger of your market. Become an expert, share your knowledge and build the credibility of your new venture, all at the same time.

CUSTOMER TESTIMONIALS

Customer testimonials are a powerful form of social proof. Try to convince customers to let you use their names and quotes on your website. If they'll post positive reviews of your products and services online, that's pure gold. Moreover, keep in mind at the start these don't have to be complete strangers. They can even be people who you offered products and services for free. As long as they're offering honest analysis and praise you can sleep well at night, knowing that the world will see your satisfied customers.

Customers also represent chances for your social proof to spread like viruses over the Internet. Twitter, Facebook, Tumblr, YouTube, Yelp, and so on are obvious targets for consumer-driven businesses but don't neglect them for business customers as well. LinkedIn and other specialty networks, as well as in-person conferences and the like, can be great opportunities to get your audience to spread the word about you on your behalf.

ACHIEVEMENT

Nothing says credibility to a customer like actual proof of your achievements. So, fulfill your promises. Meet deadlines. Stay within budgets. Set expectations low, and then blow people away with your progress. We understand that it's hard sometimes even to get that first customer---some great businesses simply have high customer acquisition costs at first---but focus on anything you can do to impress a potential customer and achieve results.

Remember, your goal is to present solutions and genuine progress. Follow these strategies in order to build credibility so you can attract resources and serve customers. You'll see a lot of competitors spend money on marketing and PR tactics that don't actually attract customers. That's mainly about ego. If you do something different---focus your effort on building your marketing and PR in a more constructive way---you'll be way ahead of the pack.

RECRUIT A CREDIBLE BOARD OF ADVISERS

Another method to generate credibility employing the techniques of authority and social proof is to build a board of advisers and a technical board. Another great but seldom-used opportunity is to create a customer advisory board, too. Who better to advise your company than representative customers?

Getting one impressive person on an advisory board can lead to another and then another. This is what we might call *springboard credibility*: Each success becomes a "win" that you can trumpet to other stakeholders, which translates into more proof your idea is good and that the team can execute. That in turn builds a platform from which to reach out for even more impressive achievements. Each step minimizes the risk profile for the next stakeholder you want to recruit, whether she's an adviser, a vendor, an investor---or even a customer.

You might ask what's in it for these advisers to join your board. In many cases entrepreneurs compensate advisors in the form of stock, although the package can vary greatly based on how attractive the company looks and at what stage they're becoming associated with it. But there are other reasons as well. Many successful people might be willing to help or lend their names to a project just because they believe in its utility. There might be a degree of vanity involved, and a simple desire to be part of something cutting edge and cool. Also, successful people who have worked very hard to earn their achievements often want to help others on the entrepreneurial journey. Helping the next generation can be an important part of their legacies.

BUSINESS EXAMPLE:
BUILDING CREDIBILITY

Two classmates and aspiring entrepreneurs, Jenifer Carter Fleiss and Jennifer Hyman, were eating lunch together. They'd spent a lot of time over the past few months talking about potential business ideas, and now they'd hit an idea they thought was perfect. Hyman described how she'd commiserated with her sister over the high cost of a dress she wanted to wear to a wedding. Suddenly it had hit her: *Why can't women rent expensive clothing for special occasions?*

Over the next few weeks, Fleiss and Hyman surveyed young professional women they knew---in other words, their potential customers. They reached out to alumnae who had become entrepreneurs and asked for advice, and they realized they had a possible introduction to one of the stars of the U.S. fashion industry, designer Diane von Furstenberg. It was an extended, friend-of-a-friend-of-a-friend connection, but they did everything they could to get von Furstenberg's personal email address. Simply meeting with her was a coup in and of itself.

By attracting people like von Furstenberg as advisers and potential business customers---and managing to convince a partner at the law firm of WilmerHale to take them on for free until they were able to raise money---they were able to pitch to Bain Capital and raise a first round of venture capital with the firm.

Their new company, called *Rent the Runway*, opened its virtual doors. Within 18 months, the company employed 31 people, had been featured twice in *The New York Times*, had raised two rounds of venture capital, and was doing great business.

Fleiss recalled that in chasing after those small wins, like winning over von Furstenberg, "both of us had developed the ability to hear no 500 times, and say, 'okay, maybe next time.'"

Each new, highly credible person who became involved made it more likely that yet another new, highly credible person or organization would be interested.

RAISING MONEY

Raising money can be an effective (though delicate) credibility milestone. Too many entrepreneurs seem to think that their goal as a founder is simply to attract investment, especially at the venture capital level. But simply raising money is never the end state of any compelling business. The goal instead is to develop a profitable venture, which requires profitably serving customers' needs. In fact, focusing exclusively on investment goes against the mantra we've returned to throughout this book: *Maximum information for minimum cost.*

Attracting investors is rarely as easy as people think it will be but, paradoxically, there are probably more sources of startup capital in the world now than ever before. We're living in what many investors consider a low-return financial world. Wealthy people and institutions have been placing their money in safe, low return investments like government bonds. Fundamentally, investors seek the best risk-adjusted returns, so if you can offer something solid and interesting, you're in better shape than you might think.

It's also important to consider what we might call the "quality" of your money and the degree to which raising money from particular investors can bolster your credibility. Like the service providers you bring aboard or contract with, the relative impressiveness of your investors can go a long way toward bolstering your credibility. Convince Warren Buffett to invest, and you know others will follow. Likewise, if you're looking for government investors, attracting the U.S. as a backer will probably earn you more credibility, than, say the government of Nigeria. The quality of your partners matters.

It's also likely that some investors will match your business better than others. For example, early investors in the ticket-trading website StubHub included Joe Montana and other professional athletes. Getting the investment was important, but having hall-of-famer athletes involved also lent the company credibility.

Securing investment is easier if you develop a business in an industry where investors are already gathering. Be careful not to do this at the expense of the things we've talked about in earlier modules, like playing to your strengths and finding real, compelling solutions to legitimate customer problems. Still, it helps to think of industries that present promise, and the places where investors are looking: renewable energy, conservation, green technology, health sciences, the Internet, and maybe some types of IT infrastructure, for example. Investors often focus on industries because there is true customer demand there. Just keep in mind that it helps to know something about a field in order to enter it in an intelligent way.

We'll talk more about approaching investors---angels, super angels, and venture capitalists---in Module 7. For now, realize that while investors might be more cautious today than they were five or ten years ago, the fact is there are more potential investors today than at any time in past decade. Money doesn't want to stay on the sidelines; it wants to get in the game.

THE BIG PICTURE

When you're raising money, ask yourself: Do you feel as if you're getting one over on the potential investor, or do you feel as if you're genuinely giving him the chance of a lifetime? When you're recruiting employees and pitching to customers, do you believe that you're truly offering them something great? The answers to these questions can be yet another gut check as to whether you've truly tested your idea and done everything you can to maximize its success. You can see why we said at the outset that if you don't absorb and apply the fundamentals of developing and testing ideas, nothing else in this book matters. You're always better off when you're in a position to offer legitimate value---not where you're trying to shore up a shoddy idea by bolstering your credibility.

If you're building something interesting, you're likely to find investors rushing to meet you in this environment. In fact, if you truly have a compelling proposition that you've tested and you find you're having trouble attracting investors, contact us. Meet the test and we'll be happy to help.

MODULE 7

"Never buy new what can be bought second-hand. Never buy what you can lease. Never lease what you can rent. Never rent what you can borrow. Never borrow what you can salvage."

-Ian MacMillian

MARSHALING RESOURCES

You're just starting out. You don't have much money. You don't have any customers. You certainly don't have any employees. Maybe you have a partner, maybe you're on your own. You're sure, however, that you have a compelling value proposition to offer---one you've tested as extensively as possible.

What do you do next? How do you gather the resources you need to get going?

Here's an inspiring example of how it's done.

Nearly universally known now as the cofounders of Google, it wasn't that long ago that Larry Page and Sergey Brin were simply smart, ambitious graduate students and friends. Their parents took pride in their academic accomplishments. Sergey's father thought--or perhaps even hoped---that one day his son would follow in his footsteps and become a university professor.

They'd met on Larry's first day at Stanford and got along so well that classmates got used to referring to them together so that their names melded into a single five-syllable word: *LarryandSergey*. They talked without end, about whatever topics entered their minds. One minute they'd discuss serious subjects like computer science or philosophy, or solving the world's transportation problems. The next minute they'd argue passionately about things that were utterly absurd--- a friend recalled Larry and Sergey's intense debate about whether it would be structurally possible to build an entire building out of lima beans. Larry's graduate student officemates learned to work with headphones on; otherwise they'd never be able to concentrate because of all the banter.

In 1996, Larry was refining his thesis plan, which involved organizing the entire World Wide Web according to how many links each page attracted from other pages. Larry and Sergey had teamed up, designed programs, and sent "spiders" across the Internet in an attempt to literally map out everything in cyberspace. This extremely ambitious project turned out to be far more difficult, time-consuming, and expensive than Larry had anticipated. He eventually estimated that each time he and Sergey launched a wandering "spider" program, it cost Stanford something like $20,000. They needed more computers, and eventually that meant they were going to need more money.

Convinced that their project would likely have commercial appeal, they decided to approach corporations and investors. They offered to license their technology to AltaVista, the top search engine at the time, for $1 million, and then to another search engine, Excite. Both companies passed. They made the rounds of venture capital firms on Sand Hill Road. Nobody was interested. The founders of Yahoo! turned them down. Larry and Sergey's project made searching the Internet too easy; Yahoo! wanted to encourage users to stay on Yahoo!, not send them elsewhere on the Web.

Passionate as they were about their work, Larry and Sergey had many other options. Silicon Valley was booming, and they could have walked away at just about any time and gone on to one of dozens of Internet companies. Yet they were sold on the elegance and utility of their project.

A friend offered to rent them the garage in her Palo Alto home for about $1,700 a month. They could swing that for a bit, but it was just the least of their expenditures. They had two of the three assets any entrepreneur needs---great people and time---but they were sorely lacking in capital. In fact, they could barely afford the computers they needed to buy in order to continue the project.

"I don't see how you're ever going to get the money," a faculty adviser told them.

"You're going to see," Larry replied. "We'll figure that out."

THE THREE RESOURCES

Whatever you are trying to achieve, remember the principle that Larry and Sergey understood even as they set out to organize the Internet from a garage in Palo Alto: There are only three fundamental resources you will be working with to achieve your entrepreneurial goals: *time, people,* and *money.* As an entrepreneur, you can usually trade one for the others.

Let's talk about what we mean by resources. Professor Howard Stevenson of Harvard Business School developed a classic definition of entrepreneurship, one that people often need to say out loud 50 or 100 times before they can really understand what it means. The definition goes something like this:

Entrepreneurship is a management style focused on the pursuit of opportunity without regard to resources currently controlled.

Take it in pieces. First, we'll be digging much deeper into the first part of that definition---what it means to say that entrepreneurship is *a management style*---in the next module. So let's set that aside for the moment.

Next, if you've read this far in this book, the second part of the definition---*pursuit of opportunity*---probably makes some sense. You've spent a lot of time on this, figuring out how to identify entrepreneurial opportunities and how to evaluate and select the most promising ones. Tactics such as identifying customer pain, calculating value propositions and market size, and the like are all geared toward helping you identify the right opportunities to pursue.

The third part is most important. It's the piece that connects an individual entrepreneur's ambition with the societal progress that results from creative destruction: *"without regard to resources currently controlled."*

Entrepreneurs need to focus on how to legally and ethically use just about any resource on the planet. Can you offer other people ways to use their assets more efficiently? Then it's your obligation to show them. This is why we devoted an entire module to talking about building credibility. It's critically important that you, as well as your stakeholders, believe with good reason that you can achieve success. That belief is what will help you obtain needed resources regardless of what you do or don't have access to at the outset.

Think about how your entrepreneurial plan can legitimately offer value to the holders of other resources. (You make the call: Would it have been a good idea for AltaVista, Excite or Yahoo! to have used a small amount of their resources to take control of Google when it was offered to them back in the late 1990s?) Of course there are key assets you'll need in order to succeed in any entrepreneurial venture---time, people, and money--- but the important thing to remember is that you don't need to control those resources at the start. In fact, it can hurt you to have the resources too early, because you might lose the motivation to test your ideas cheaply at the start.

Even if you never actually start a new venture, this simple point can still change your life. Every time you want to make any important decision, there are two possible courses of action. You can look at the array of choices that present themselves, pick the best available option and try to make it fit. Or, you can do what the true entrepreneur does: Figure out the best conceivable option and then make it available.

So, how do you create options? As Professor Stevenson suggests, how do you gather together resources that you don't currently control? We'll explore that issue below, but for inspiration, let's first round out the early days of the Google story.

Larry and Sergey kept pushing. A Stanford professor, David Cheriton, made an introduction for them and they had a chance to pitch their idea to an investor named Andy Bechtolsheim, who had been one of the cofounders of Sun Microsystems. Bechtolsheim met with the young co-founders at Cheriton's house, and before the morning was out, he was sold.

"This is the single best idea I have heard in years," he told them. "I want to be a part of this."

There was no haggling over terms and conditions, no debate over what the company was worth or what his stake in it would be. Bechtolsheim simply wrote a check for $100,000 to Google, Inc., which was more than enough to buy the computers and other things they needed to continue their work.

Just like that, Larry and Sergey had their seed money. Now all they had to do was incorporate a company called Google so they could open a bank account. Bechtolsheim's check sat in Larry's desk drawer for two weeks before they had a chance to deposit it. They were too busy mapping the Internet.

THE FIRST RESOURCE: TIME

Would-be entrepreneurs often think that they're held back by lack of money or perhaps lack of the right people. In truth, however, the scarcest asset of all is time. It takes time simply to brainstorm and test entrepreneurial ideas. Moreover, if you start a company and it's successful, there's little doubt that it will consume you.

"You can't say, 'I'm really smart, but I'm not going to work the long hours,'" explained billionaire and super angel investor Ram Shriram, who became a major Google investor early on as well as the company's founding board member. He'd also been a senior executive at Amazon. "It needs to be sort of self-directional, self-inspired, and something that others can look up to."

Time, people, or money: that's all it comes down to. So, how do you get more time? Quit your day job? Dedicate your evenings and weekends? In truth, you probably will do this, at least to some degree, especially in the early stages of your venture. But working insane hours is usually something people can only do temporarily. They burn out. So it's critical for the entrepreneur to take two actions regarding time. The first action is to increase the time available, which can usually only be done by growing the team (and thus the available person-hours). The second action is to manage your time very effectively.

We'll talk about expanding your team in the next section, but for now, how does the savvy entrepreneur manage time? The smartest way to do that is to ensure each day that you identify tangible objectives to accomplish, with a special focus on things that help you assess (or eliminate) business or technical risk.

Achieve, and hold yourself accountable. Do you remember what gerunds are, from high school English class? They're verbs that end with "-ing," such as *talking, working, considering*, and the like. As an entrepreneur, they're your silent time-killing enemy. The only verbs you need to be concerned with as an entrepreneur are those in the future tense---things you will do---and those in the past tense--- things you have already achieved.

So, avoid spending your day *doing* things like *making* phone calls, *holding* meetings and *brainstorming* or *considering* options. God forbid that you look back at the end of the day and have to acknowledge that you spent hours *checking* your email or *surfing* the Internet. Keep a schedule. Use checklists at the end of the day, so that you can force yourself to record honestly how you spent your time. Put together a Gantt chart so that you can maintain focus on the big picture and see how what you do each day impacts it.

Responsible people with limited financial budgets tend to be strict about their spending. As an entrepreneur you have a limited time budget. So you must be absolutely focused and ruthless about how you spend your time. This might all sound harsh, but a successful entrepreneur needs to work a lot---and he or she needs to work effectively.

The Second Resource: People

It's not impossible to find good people, but it's very hard to find the *right* people. Great teams have to have complementary skills. In almost all successful ventures, they truly know and understand each other, on a personal level.

Stories of successful teams who form without really knowing each other---who find each other on Craigslist or the like---are more likely myth than reality.

"I always find the team before the idea," explained investor and entrepreneur In Sik Rhee, who co-founded two successful startups, including Opsware, which was acquired by Hewlett Packard for $1.6 billion, and Kiva, which was acquired by Netscape for $180 million. "That's something that I always ask entrepreneurs. Which came first? Did you come up with the idea first? Or did you find your co-founders? I think that is 'step zero' in the process."

In other words, before you try to build a company, it's helpful to have spent a few hours debating with your cofounder whether you could build a building out of lima beans---or whatever your equivalent might be.

"It's fundamentally important that you have teammates that you can trust," Rhee continued. "Most founding teams are born of people who have history together. Whether it's college buddies, or roommates, or [people who] worked in the same company... When I see start-ups fall apart, it's because of the lack of inter-team trust. You have founders who don't know enough about the other partners, and constantly have to double-check, triple-check and question their decision-making or executions. A startup can't afford that."

Clearly, friendship and the relationship aren't quite enough, though. You want co-founders who refuse to fail. You want people who are capable and follow through. Pick triathletes, not couch potatoes. Talk to as many of their personal contacts as you can. Find examples of what they've done in the past. Do trial work before you really commit. Again, it's hard to find better examples in this regard than Sergey Brin and Larry Page, who worked together on an academic project for many months before they considered launching a company.

It's also critically important to find additional team members with complementary skill sets.

"That's how you craft a story for investors," Rhee continued. "Investors want to see a team, they want to see two or three guys.

You know, 'Henry here is a brilliant techie and a computer scientist... but then I need Justin here to explain to me the value that we're going to provide for the market, and then I need Simon here to knock on doors and close them into actual revenue deals ... You want to get a set of players. You don't want [founders who are] four engineers in a room, all writing code," regardless of how brilliant they are and how much they trust each other.

Matt Szulik, the co-founder and former CEO of Red Hat, agreed. "Good-quality industrialists will look at the experience curve, they will look at the level of interest, the history of innovation, the history of leadership of the founders. They'll ask for demonstrations of when that passion has been demonstrated ... They'll look at the value systems. Are these people honorable? Do they have integrity? Do they tell the truth?"

Szulik talked about an investment he'd made in one company in particular, where one of the founders called him late at night to say he'd taken out a second mortgage on his house to help fund the company.

"'I don't want you to ever think that I'm not committed to this,'" Szulik remembered the founder telling him. "He didn't need to do this, hypothetically, but I think he wanted to make a statement about his long-term commitment to this enterprise and I think it's very rare."

Because he demonstrated that kind of commitment and integrity, Szulik said, "he has my undying loyalty now."

BEYOND THE FOUNDERS

Not everyone gets to be a founder. You'll likely need to add additional employees, independent contractors, and other team members. When you're thinking about the people you need to add---and the roles you need to fill---start by focusing on these five functions:

- Product development

- Sales

- Production and delivery

- Marketing

- Internal operations

Product development and *sales* are tied for first among equals, because they directly work on solving the problems of technical risk and business risk, respectively. Production and delivery flow from there. Marketing, in turn, is a function in partnership with sales--- branding, figuring out features, pricing, developing customer leads, etc.

To find people who can achieve all of these functions, you can follow a five-step process:

- First, focus on job function. Figure out which of the five functions you most urgently need to address.

- Second, write a description of what role this person will play.

- Third, generate a pool of candidates through methods we'll discuss below.

- Fourth, apply your selection criteria and choose the best candidate.

- Finally, get your new team members up to speed on your venture and its goals.

Your cofounders, we hope, will be people you already know. But when you need to expand your team, where do you look? In descending order of efficacy, here are five worthwhile strategies to pursue.

WORD OF MOUTH & PERSONAL RELATIONSHIPS

Personal relationships are likely the best way to find great people, presuming you can identify candidates with the skill sets that you need. You want to have the best opportunity to evaluate them informally---to scrounge information about them. Either you'll know them and have been able to observe them in many settings, or else you'll be able to ask people you know and trust about them. Think of some of the great founding teams. Sixty years before Larry Page and Sergey Brin, Bill Hewlett and Dave Packard, co-founders of the company that bears their names, were classmates at Stanford. Steve Jobs and Steve Wozniak of Apple were friends and fellow computer hobbyists. Bill Gates and Paul Allen were childhood friends. Chad Hurley, Steve Chen, and Jawad Karim of YouTube were all former coworkers at PayPal. Jerry Yang and David Filo were graduate student classmates at Stanford before launching Yahoo!. There are going to be times in a startup when the participants will each anger, disappoint and maybe even enrage each other. You need a common frame of reference and the experience of working well with each other in the past, so you can weather the rough times in the future.

REFERRALS FROM OTHER EMPLOYEES

One step removed from your personal and professional relationships, you'll want to leverage your partners' and employees' relationships. If you've hired one techie or salesperson who works well with you, for example, use that person to recruit others he or she has worked with before. Harvard Business School Professor William Sahlman puts it this way: "You want to recruit someone who <u>knows</u> the industry and who is also <u>known</u> in the industry." This doesn't just apply to large companies or technical fields; in fact, it's probably even more important in smaller markets to recruit someone your customers already know. So if you want to recruit a new engineer, ask the engineers you've already recruited. You'll likely find your best new employees by asking your best existing employees for referrals.

GO WHERE THEY ARE

If you want to recruit a great technical person, for example, go where the tech people hang out---either in person or virtually. This could mean recruiting at colleges and universities, or else from alumni associations. There are online forums and message boards that attract people in specific fields and trade shows and associations to target. For that matter, if you need a person who specializes in a particular function, there's usually nothing wrong with figuring out who excels in that job at another company, calling him or her up, and trying to hire them away.

Think back to the key, life-changing rule: Don't just pick the best available option; figure out what the best option could conceivably be, and put your mind to creating it for yourself. In this context, you could run a job ad and pick from the candidates who respond (i.e., the best available options), or, you can go to where the best people you want hang out, and target them there (i.e., identify the best person and work to make him or her available).

NETWORK IN REAL TIME

Taking that idea to another level, one HR recruiter we know talks about a strategy he calls "networking in real time." When he has a job he wants to fill, he looks up people on LinkedIn who already hold that position at other firms, calls them and asks if they'd be interested to think about a new opportunity. If they aren't interested, he thanks them for their time---and then asks if they can recommend 2 or 3 colleagues who *might* be interested. Then he'll call those people, and repeat the process: if they're not interested he asks them for the names of two or three people who might be. Spend a day doing this, and as long as you've taken the lessons of the first six modules of this book to heart, odds are you'll wind up interviewing some very promising candidates.

RUN ADVERTISEMENTS

Many of us, if we were looking for a job, might instinctively start the search by logging on to one of the Internet job boards and searching to see what is available. But there are drawbacks for both the employer and the job applicant in this model. There's only so much you can learn about each other based on a few written materials like a resume, a job description, and a one-hour interview.

That's not to say the sites are without value. Sometimes you might need to move especially quickly to hire someone. Alternatively, one very successful entrepreneur we know (who wanted to remain anonymous) needed to hire a vice-president of engineering at the outset of his company---his first real product development specialist. However, he didn't really know much about this particular subspecialty of software engineering. His solution? He went on Monster.com, searched for vice presidents of engineering, and started looking at resumes. Over time, he cut and pasted their backgrounds, erased the names, generalized their experience and education, and edited it all into a job description that he ran as his own Monster ad.

In other words, he reverse-engineered his ideal vice president of engineering. After many, many interviews, he hired the perfect candidate.

EVALUATING CANDIDATES

If you've found the right place to look, what exactly are you looking for? Just as when you evaluate potential cofounders, there are three essential questions you need to answer when considering any potential hire:

- Can they do the job?

- Will they do the job?

- Will they fit the culture of the organization?

First off, *how do you know if they can do the job?* If you're a subject-matter expert, of course, you can ask for samples of work and evaluate them. Give them hypothetical challenges to solve and pay as much attention to how they address the problem as the solution they come up with. Give them homework between interviews. Heck, ask them to complete a project before the first interview, if you like.

But, what do you do if you don't have the foggiest idea about their field? How does an engineer hire a marketer? How does a salesperson hire a technical expert? In a word, by scrounging. Our entrepreneur friend who mashed up engineers' resumes to create a job description realized he didn't quite have the background to interview candidates intelligently at first. So, when the first candidate came in, he started out by describing the web application that he wanted to build and asked the candidate how he'd do it. The interviewer took furious notes. When the second and third candidates came in, he asked the same questions, and used what he'd learned from the first interview to challenge their ideas. By the time he got to the 25th or 30th candidate, he might not have known everything about the field---but he knew a lot more than when he began, and it was enough to hire an excellent employee.

Next up, *will they do the job?* Here, you're looking for motivation. How committed are the potential candidates? Why are they excited to work for or with you? You want to know about their work ethic, their honesty, and their attitude. Ask them tough questions. Force them to express their likes and dislikes, the things they're passionate about and the things they want nothing to do with. For example, you could describe three hypothetical projects, and ask them to rank which they'd most and least like to work on, and why. If the project they say they'd least enjoy happens to be something you want this candidate to do, maybe it will lead you to decide they'd be happier elsewhere.

You'll want to check references, of course, but not just the ones the candidate provides. You can contact their old employers and colleagues, even their old teachers or professors. The federal government investigates ten or more years into an applicant's past for even the most routine jobs. Shouldn't you do a similar check on the people you're trusting with your new venture's future? Conducting this kind of due diligence on potential employees might surprise a few candidates, but the ones you really want on your team will be impressed. As President Ronald Reagan used to say, "trust but verify."

Will they fit in? This is the most difficult part of the search to evaluate. It's hard to describe in a checklist because you need to see your candidate in different situations. Often, it's not until someone has truly gone through the interview process, accepted the job, come aboard, and worked with you for a little while that you truly start to learn who they really are. Still, you want to get as much information as you can ahead of time.

Matt Szulik of Red Hat follows an interesting strategy to obtain this kind of information ahead of time. He's convinced that people decide early in their lives what level of success they want to achieve.

"For some people, it's academic. They want to get a Ph.D. from Cal-Berkeley. For others, it's athletic. They want to be team captain or they want to be a pro athlete. Others, it could be they want to be the CEO of Google. And along the way, they make decisions at every step that would re-affirm the commitment to themselves and the pursuit of those goals," he explained.

So, during an interview, Szulik simply asks them what they think "successful" means, and how they've tried to achieve it.

"It's amazing how fast 60 minutes can get filled, as an interviewer, by keeping your mouth shut and asking people to tell you their life's journey as they've created their success model," Szulik said. "I find that to be completely binary. The ones that have it can take you on a fantastic journey. The ones that don't---who say, 'You know what, I never really thought about that,'---cannot."

It seems so simple, but merely asking questions like these helps job candidates help you, by making your hiring decisions much easier.

THE THIRD RESOURCE: MONEY

Money is a resource. It's not the goal. Every time you raise money, you'll give up a degree of ownership in your venture, so unless you're getting something really good in return, you should be wary. We're certainly not saying, 'never raise money,' but recognize that at some early stage, every company in the world was self-financed. On the other end of the funding spectrum, the percentage of companies that ever get venture capital funding is very small. That's perfectly fine.

A detailed examination of entrepreneurial finance is the topic of another book, but broadly---very broadly---for every round of financing, you'll likely give up a third to half of your company. There are many exceptions and many other deal points you'll need to be aware of: shareholder rights and different classes of stock, for example, can make all the difference in a deal. So, as we hope you're not planning to end your entrepreneurial education after reading *Breakthrough Entrepreneurship*, we can refer you to many other resources, such as *Entrepreneurial Finance: A Casebook* by Paul Gompers and Bill Sahlman.

With that said, what are your funding options?

SELF-FUNDING

Nearly everybody self-funds to some degree. When you make that first call or do the first Google search on your personal laptop trying to estimate your market size---congratulations, you've joined the ranks of the self-funded entrepreneurs. In truth, a sizeable majority of entrepreneurs never get past the self-funding phase, whether they're successful or not.

There are pros and cons to being self-funded. On the one hand, you maintain the most control, and there's very little paperwork involved (except maybe for your monthly personal credit card bill). If things work out fantastically, you don't have to share the windfall with anyone else. You also don't have to convince anyone else of your idea to begin with.

On the other hand, the cons start with the same things: If things go poorly, you've concentrated both your money and time. You don't have a sounding board because you didn't have to convince anyone else in order to get started. Having checks and balances can often lead to a better outcome.   In this day and age you can get relatively far without putting too much money into many businesses, but keep in mind that you want to get maximum information for minimum cost.   Perhaps the best strategy is to limit your spending until you're certain you're onto a good idea and then attempt to raise outside investment.

There is one more important aspect of self-funding to consider. Many entrepreneurs wind up self-funding their businesses by going into debt.   Virtually any lender will require an entrepreneur--- especially a first-time entrepreneur---to provide collateral for a loan. Follow this route and you can wind up mortgaging the house, running up credit card debt, or taking a margin loan.   It's risky business---and we don't mean the Tom Cruise kind. So yet again: Get maximum information early, for minimum cost.

BOOTSTRAPPING

A few lucky entrepreneurs start businesses that are self-funded by profits from the business itself.   In other words, the business actually generates sufficient cash to fund its own growth.   The advantages here are pretty similar to that of self-funding: you don't need to share the windfall, and you don't need to concede control or convince anyone else. The difference, perhaps, is that if you're able to bootstrap then that's a pretty solid indication that you're right about your idea's merits, at least in the short term.

This is in many ways the optimal financing strategy. Much of this book is intended to push you toward a bootstrap model, or at least push you toward a position from which it's truly an option. Of course, remember that your growth opportunities will be constrained by how much cash your company generates.

That said, this can be a wonderful form of financing, albeit a rare one. In order to bootstrap, keep expenses smart and low, test ideas first, and get that cash.

FRIENDS AND FAMILY

As you decide to raise more money, the first place you might turn is to your friends and family---the people closest to you. There are some advantages, of course. These are the people who already trust you, and it might be easier to convince them than it would be to convince an unknown entity to back you. It could be advantageous that they want to be a part of things and help out, and maybe it's a way for them to get involved. A lot really depends on the relationships you have with them beforehand.

Once again, though the downside is identical. They're more likely to stick with you through tough times, but if you borrow thousands of dollars from your parents or other relatives and things go sour---well, count on some tense Thanksgiving dinners. Moreover, consider the flipside: What if you are eventually very successful, but you refused to let your family or friends invest? A number of successful entrepreneurs hold fast to the rule that family and business don't mix, while others make it work quite well. Your mileage may vary.

NONPROFESSIONAL ANGEL INVESTORS

Moving beyond your friends and family, you might next go to a "nonprofessional angel," an individual person with sufficient wealth who might be willing to invest in your venture. A good rule of thumb would be someone who qualifies at the least to be an accredited investor under SEC rules (meaning generally that they have had at least $200,000 in income for two years running).

There are many would-be investors out there who can write a check for $100,000 to $200,000, so there are a lot of options. Nonprofessional angels might not try to micromanage you too much---although there's always a danger that they might not know anything about the business but try to micromanage you anyway. You might be taking on yet another marriage partner, so to speak, in addition to your cofounders and your real-life marriage or relationship partners. That can really complicate a company.

EXPERIENCED ANGELS/GROUPS OF ANGELS

Next up, you can go to an experienced angel investor or groups of angels---your own personal Andy Bechtolsheim, for example. There are lots of angel groups out there: YCombinator and Band of Angels, to name a few. You can check out Angelsoft.net and, for about $200, put together a pitch for angels either in your local area or across the country. As for individual angels, you might be targeting a manager at a public company like Google who got in early and who has the ability to put up $100,000 for a new venture.

Typically bands of angels have industry expertise, will have invested in many businesses before, and probably have a formal evaluation process. The difficult side is that they're probably more sophisticated financially than you are. They'll have more influence and control than you expect---although that can be a positive, too, if they bring not just money, but also contacts and experience. In the best cases, groups of angels act almost like additional cofounders---smart people who have a significant stake in the company and who want it to succeed. You provide sweat equity while they provide financial equity. It can be an excellent arrangement when it works well.

SUPER ANGELS

This is a newer class of investors: Individuals who can invest significant amounts of capital that may be comparable to the size of investments made by traditional venture capital firms. One example is Ram Shrirarm, whom we quoted earlier in this module, or Ron Conway, another of the early stage investors in Google who made enormous profits and has since invested in a large number of other startups.

On the plus side, these are typically investors with good track records, and with an entrepreneurial process in place.

On the negative side, though, they're likely investing in many companies, so you don't know how much attention you'll receive. Moreover, they're very sophisticated investors, so you'd better make sure you understand entrepreneurial finance---or at least that your advisers and lawyers do----before you sign a term sheet.

VENTURE CAPITAL

Venture capital firms invest large pools of money, and they do so in a very process-oriented manner. They're funded most often by pension funds, endowments, and high-net-worth-individuals. The firms can be as small as $50 million and range up to billions of dollars. Typically, VC firms will want to invest between $10 million and $30 million in each company, often over multiple rounds of financing. They're concentrated in Silicon Valley and Boston, with some in Austin, Chicago, Los Angeles, and a few other areas, all chasing after what are a relatively small number of new ideas with true potential.

The positive side is that there are some firms with lots of experience that can make sizeable investments. The downside is that for these folks, making money off of startups is their business. They might be great partners in building your business, but when the time comes to extract value, rest assured they'll be great at that, too! Compared with an individual accredited investor, they might offer a lot more to make you successful---but they'll likely take a lot more in return.

If you decide to approach a venture capital investor, do so through a person already known by the firm you're targeting. Often this means a lawyer, or perhaps a well-respected entrepreneur or industry figure---maybe somebody you've recruited to your board of advisers. These firms receive a huge number of business plans each year and they will typically only read proposals referred to them by someone they already know.   Some important advice that bears repeating: Think about investors as a means to an end. Your company may require capital to start and grow. You may also receive advice and genuine partnership from savvy investors. But raising money is never the goal in and of itself. The entrepreneur's objective is to solve customer pain and pursue opportunity.

PROTECTING INTELLECTUAL PROPERTY

Entrepreneurs often worry about someone else taking their ideas as they go out to recruit team members and raise money. You might reasonably ask yourself, what can I do to protect these hard-won assets? This is an important question, but an equally important one is, how have you protected against someone claiming that you've based your business on *their* intellectual property? Potential stakeholders will want to know what defenses you've put in place.

As we explore a few of these areas, we have to caution you not to take what we're saying here as legal advice. If you have a highly technical business idea, or you're preoccupied with protecting intellectual property that you think is the core of your business, you should factor a budget for professional legal advice into your early plan.

At the same time, for most entrepreneurs, the risk that someone will steal your idea before you get going is usually much smaller than the risk that you won't ever get started at all. It's fairly rare that you'll pitch a business idea to an investor who will steal your idea, cut you out of the deal, and start up with someone else instead. That said, there is one exception, and it explains why you should do what you can to know everything possible about who you're pitching to ahead of time. If you were to pitch to sophisticated investors who had already invested in (or were talking seriously with) a competing firm, you can pretty much rest assured that everything of interest that you say to the potential investors will be shared with your competitor.

Again, if you're truly working on a business that has a lot of intellectual property issues, then you need to hire a lawyer. At the same time, though, that whole "maximum information for minimum cost" idea pretty much goes out the window as soon as the lawyers show up. So if you don't have $20,000 to spend at the outset on legal fees, what should you do before you call a lawyer and spend money?

There are three main intellectual property questions that you should at least be aware of---*trademark, copyright,* and *patents.* There's also the catch-all issue of *who owns intellectual property that you might have developed while you were employed by somebody else?*

TRADEMARK

A trademark is a name, sign, or other indication used to signify that products or services originate from a particular source. To be effective, a trademark has to be distinct from other trademarks, not prohibited or generic, and not so descriptive or universal that it can't be reasonably reserved for one company. As an example, The Coca-Cola Company claims trademarks including Coke, Coca-Cola, The Real Thing, and hundreds of others, but it probably couldn't have trademarked the words "soda" or "pop." Likewise, Google goes to great lengths to try to ensure that the word "Google" does not become simply a synonym for "search on the Internet."

There are both state and federal trademarks, and you can hire firms that will search trademarks for you. In this day and age, however, it might be possible to do at least the bare minimum yourself. Of course, you can Google your proposed trademark (er, we mean, do a search on Google for your proposed trademark), or else look to see if anyone has already registered and used a domain name based on your proposed trademark. You don't want to limit your search to exact matches, however. Basically anything that's close enough to be reminiscent of another company's mark or product could create a trademark violation. For example, if you wanted to start a car rental company, you obviously couldn't call it Zipcar, because that name is already trademarked. But you also probably couldn't call it "Zingcar," or "Zipauto," or anything else that would likely confuse consumers.

Additionally, keep in mind that it's not just words that can be trademarked. Logos, designs, and even colors or shapes can be trademarked as well. We wouldn't recommend trying to start a car company that used a blue oval for its logo (like Ford) or a computer company that used the silhouette of a fruit for its symbol (like Apple).

Generally, the more original and distinctive your trademark is, the easier it will be to obtain and defend. To take legal steps to protect your trademark, set aside about $400 to register it with the U.S. Patent and Trademark Office website. You can find services that will do the paperwork for you for another $150 to $200.

COPYRIGHT

A copyright is a form of protection under U.S. law for "original works of authorship" such as books, sound recordings, plays, paintings, and software. Generally, you don't have to do much to ensure that you have a copyright in your created works, as copyright protection is automatic when the work is fixed in a tangible form of expression---namely when it is written down, painted, or recorded. At least in the United States, simply the act of creating also establishes a copyright for the lifetime of the creator plus 70 years. Although you are not required to register your work with the U.S. Patent and Trademark Office in order for it to be protected, registration is recommended. It puts the world on notice that you own the copyright on the work and makes it easier to defend if someone infringes on you. Registration is relatively straightforward, and the USPTO has forms online to assist you.

However, you do have to be cognizant of the copyrights others claim in things you might try to use. This is an especially big deal if you're somehow using or even selling other people's intellectual property. In modern times, this might be something to consider, especially if you want to launch an Internet venture that will leverage a lot of user-generated content. Suppose you were to create a dating site---can you use your members' descriptions of themselves in your advertising? It's advisable to consult with a lawyer as you draft terms of service. At the very least, familiarized yourself with the terms of service used by the big ventures in this field ahead of time.

PATENTS

A patent is a set of rights granted by the government to an inventor in exchange for the inventor's sharing the invention with the public. The inventor has the right to exclude others from using the patented machine or object for 20 years, which means the inventor also has a monopolistic right to produce and sell the patented product for 20 years. If you are building a company that depends on patents, then you really do need a lawyer. There's little upside to filing patents yourself (although people do it all the time). The problem isn't that you can't figure out how to describe the state of the art, it's that you might not understand deficiencies in your application, even if it's accepted, until many years after the fact. In many business areas, you might find out the hard way that so-called patent trolls, companies that buy up patents specifically to sue potential infringers, might consider you a juicy target. Also, we're focusing here on United States patents but we're in a global market, so you have to be aware of how much deference foreign competitors will pay to an American patent. Rest assured, if you create an innovative, successful new product, you'll see blatant patent-infringers from overseas entering the game pretty quickly!

Of all the intellectual property issues you'll face, patents can be the most complicated and expensive to deal with. But once again: scrounge. It's not necessarily the case that you have to lay out tens of thousands of dollars in legal fees upfront. Rather, if you're just starting out and trying to obtain maximum information for minimum cost, you can often find an attorney who might be willing to defer payment until after you raise money.

Nondisclosure Agreements

Aspiring entrepreneurs often want to know how to get potential stakeholders to sign nondisclosure agreements. In truth, you almost never can, certainly not at first. It's hard to imagine you'll make a great impression on investors, for example, if the first thing you do is whip out a piece of paper that threatens to sue them if they behave in a particular way. (In fact it's more likely that you'll be the one signing a waiver.) Now, if you get to a later meeting in which you expect to be asked to reveal things that you could consider legitimate trade secrets, then perhaps it will be time to get a lawyer and draft an NDA.

Moreover, NDAs and other forms of protecting ideas for companies that haven't even launched yet are often effectively useless for the vast majority of would-be entrepreneurs. Even if you have a legal right to enforce an NDA, how are you going to sue somebody who takes your unproven idea? You're either going to have to run up massive legal fees or convince a lawyer that you can prove very high damages. That's hard to do if you never proved you could get the company off the ground yourself.

Your Current Employer: A Cautionary Tale

There's one more intellectual property issue you need to be aware of. It's imperative that you don't launch a company only to find out that your current employer can claim that you developed your intellectual property---or even the ideas---while you were "on the clock" for them. An important question to consider here is what you signed when started working for your employer. Did you enter into a noncompete agreement that requires you not to engage in a similar business for a particular length of time? Did you sign a "work-for-hire" agreement so that everything you created while working for your employer is considered the employer's intellectual property?

Remember, you don't want to merely put yourself in a position where you could probably win a lawsuit. You want to completely avoid these gray areas as best you can, because no entrepreneur wants to spend resources defending against lawsuits. There may be no more sure-fire way to kill an otherwise promising new venture.

Here's an example of how this can go wrong. In 2001, a California toy and game company called MGA came out with its most successful product: a line of dolls called Bratz. Bratz were sort of like big-headed Barbies (made by rival Mattel) with big attitudes. This similarity was not surprising to Mattel, since Bratz was dreamed up by a Mattel employee named Carter Bryant---allegedly while he was still working for the company.

So, who truly owns Bratz? That question has been reverberating through the federal courts in California for years now---ever since Bratz started doing something like $2 billion in business a year and cutting deeply into Mattel's market share. So far, Mattel has won one federal lawsuit against MGA over Bratz, but that case was overturned on appeal. So, they went back to retry the case while MGA filed a countersuit against Mattel...

Blah, blah, blah, blah, blah.

We don't know whether MGA stole Mattel's intellectual property, and for our purposes, it hardly matters. It does provide an important lesson, however: If you'd rather run a profitable business---instead of helping *a bunch of lawyers* run a profitable business---be aware of your intellectual property rights (and potential lack thereof!).

THE BIG PICTURE

Remember the last part of the Harvard Business School definition of entrepreneurship: *"regardless of resources currently controlled."*

They're beautiful, inspiring words. If you believe Joseph Schumpeter was onto something, then take heart. Entrepreneurs are outsiders, and by definition they normally don't have the resources at the outset that they need to turn their ideas into enterprises. However, our free market system requires the work of outsiders who spur real progress by overcoming seemingly insurmountable odds. By pursuing opportunity you can help society at large better allocate its resources.

Most of the great success stories that we celebrate in entrepreneurship started with one or two insightful founders, alone in a room with an idea. Let that inspire you and follow their examples.

In the summer of 1998, Google was comprised of an interesting idea, two smart friends, a rented garage, and a six-figure check that they couldn't even cash right away. What happened between then and now? Like every entrepreneurial success story, it's a matter of time, people, and money. Marshaling the right resources is equaled only, perhaps, by the entrepreneur's ability to manage those resources effectively. That's what we'll explore in the next module.

MODULE 8

"Management is efficiency in climbing the ladder of success; leadership determines whether the ladder is leaning against the right wall."

- **Stephen Covey**

LEARNING TO LEAD

You've got your great idea and maybe even a few customers. You've convinced some investors to take a hard look and maybe even put up some money. Perhaps you have a few employees or a couple of interns, people who look up to you and expect that some of your genius will rub off on them. At the very least, you've probably got a partner or two, and maybe some outside vendors waiting to sell you some of the things you'll need to execute your plan.

Suddenly, you're faced with a key question, one you'll be asking yourself over and over: *How do I lead these people?* Marshaling resources is important, but how do true entrepreneurs manage resources once they have them?

They say that if you want to lead, you must first learn to follow. So put yourself in the shoes of an employee at one of the most successful companies in the world: Wal-Mart. Imagine you're a hotshot young retail executive with a reputation for making great deals and cutting costs and you've just been recruited to a new job. You're eager to hit the ground running and you take it as a vote of confidence just a few weeks into the new assignment, when your boss says he wants you to fly with him to meet one of the company's biggest vendors.

You've always handled your own travel arrangements, so you book yourself on an inexpensive morning flight that will get you into town two hours before the meeting. You ask your boss what hotel he prefers. He mentions a budget chain you associate with long-haul truckers and the founders of early-stage startups, but you think to yourself, *"When in Rome..."*

You reserve a couple of rooms. A quick Internet search reveals a well-reviewed restaurant in the city you're headed to. You make a reservation, thinking you can get a nice dinner with your new boss and maybe even bond a bit while you're on the road.

You're in for a surprise. A few days before you leave, a travel manager calls to say he's changed your flight to one that leaves at 6 a.m., and he's put you in a middle seat in coach (to save $40 on the fare). He warns that your travel allowance is just $25 a day, so dinner at Chez François is probably out of reach. The biggest shock, however, is that he can't understand why you reserved two hotel rooms.

Wal-Mart employees have doubled-up in Motel-6s and La Quinta Inns across the country for decades. It's part of the legacy of Wal-Mart's founder, Sam Walton, who grew the chain from a single store into the largest retail brand in America, remaking the entire industry in the process. Two key factors contributed to his success. First, Wal-Mart developed innovative ways to track and control inventory. Second, Walton relentlessly drove prices down---by negotiating tough deals with suppliers, and by keeping costs as low as possible. Doubling up his employees in hotel rooms is tangible evidence of this legacy.

Along the way, Walton amassed the largest fortune in America, although he insisted it had never really been about the money---at least not after he'd reached a certain level of wealth and comfort. He drove an old pickup truck and he enjoyed pointing out his cheap clothing and shoes, which he picked up in his own store. He was legendary for borrowing spare change from other executives. Yet his employees loved him for it, because under his leadership they grew the company into a behemoth.

So put yourself back in the shoes of that new employee. You climb into bed the night before your trip, grumbling more than a little about having to share a motel room with your boss. The company's parsimonious attitude toward travel certainly drives home the message about managing resources effectively. You set the alarm for 4 a.m. so you'll be up in time for your cheap, early flight, and you wonder: *What the heck have I gotten myself into?* But the fact remains, you go along.

LEADING PEOPLE AND MANAGING RESOURCES
IN A NEW VENTURE

A leader faces a stark choice at the outset of an entrepreneurial venture. You need to find your personal leadership style (to the degree it is a choice) from among a spectrum of possibilities. Let's think about two of the major paths that you can choose to follow. The first is a relatively decentralized approach to leading people and managing resources that we'll refer to here as an *empowering leader*. The second is a much more centralized and controlling approach, which for sake of brevity we'll refer to as an *assertive leader*.

In ventures of all sizes and at all stages, empowering leaders take stock of the breadth and depth of the talent they've assembled. They remind themselves that nobody knows all the answers and they seek to lead by building consensus and squeezing every bit of knowledge, wisdom, and drive possible out of the people on their team. An assertive leader, on the other hand, starts by laying out his or her vision and insisting that the people he or she has attracted to the venture adhere to the goals---and even the methods--- that the leader expects.

The empowering leadership model offers some advantages. The leader doesn't need to do everything alone. Moreover, he or she can appoint people with the most knowledge and experience in each area of the business and let them do what they do best. It's this kind of decentralization and simplification that stands at the core of some of the best-regarded business leadership and strategy experts' advice. They recognize that people work most efficiently over the long term when they have efficient, established processes that allow every team member to contribute his or her all.

For all those benefits, however, there is a major drawback to the empowering leadership model in the context of a dynamic, high-growth organization like the new venture you plan to launch. As a budding entrepreneur, you likely don't have the luxury of making the long-term your top priority. While you've done your best to marshal the resources you need to get going, the truth is that you'll almost certainly face significant constraints in terms of time, people, and money. You're going to have do find ways to do more with less than your competitors do.

The Obligation of Entrepreneurial Leadership

A startup is all about managing a highly fluid situation. That usually demands a strong-willed, assertive leader---or, at most, a very small group of leaders. If you've adhered to the framework we've presented so far in this book, then you have earned the right to be an *assertive leader*. In fact, you might well have the obligation to lead in that manner.

Let's use an analogy from the investment world to help think about leadership styles. Investors can beat the market in one of two ways. Either they can obtain unique information, or they can figure out a unique way of analyzing the information that everybody has access to. There are legitimate ways to obtain unique information, of course. If you've tested ideas, for example, and done some of the kinds of independent research we advocate, then you've created an advantage as an entrepreneur. Again, this is why it is so important to follow the advice in the first several modules of this book. Nothing else matters if you haven't obtained valid data and insights that others don't have access to.

Now, we've seen since the start of our exploration of entrepreneurship that unfortunately many new ventures launch without any true, tested insight into what the market wants, what problem their venture proposes to solve, or how valuable their proposed product or service is. On a large scale, therefore, the people studying these kinds of phenomenon and investing in ventures must presume that *at best* everyone can access the *same* information. The result is that they focus largely on smarter ways to process information.

This makes plenty of sense for larger companies in established industries. It's not as if Procter & Gamble is likely to develop a unique insight about, say, social networking. More likely, they have built a solid, predictable management structure that can make incremental improvements to existing products such as Tide laundry detergent. That's fine. It's what they're structured to achieve. In fact, their shareholders likely want that kind of predictability. You don't want to invest a pension fund in a game of blackjack.

But you're not Procter & Gamble. As an entrepreneur, you are continually trying to develop unique information: Where does the unmet customer pain lie? How can you improve your value proposition? How large is the market? Once you've developed those insights, the appropriate management style isn't one where you leverage everyone's talents to design a process to manage resources. Instead, we believe the appropriate management style is one where you act more like a coach, a ship captain, or a military commander.

SAM WALTON & LEADERSHIP

Certainly we encourage you to treat your team with dignity and respect. If you don't trust your people and respect their abilities you probably shouldn't have recruited them in the first place. But startups need leaders whose force of will can ignite the company. Moreover, sometimes treating people with respect can be entirely consistent with being a taskmaster. Listen to the others on your team? Absolutely. But at the end of the day, the assertive entrepreneur can't be afraid to sound the bugle and charge.

All of which brings us back to our opening example: Sam Walton. A native of Oklahoma and a 1940 graduate of the University of Missouri, Walton worked in the management-training program at J.C. Penney's department stores before serving in the military during World War II. Afterward, he bought a franchise in the Ben Franklin chain of discount stores in Arkansas. Through insightful focus and hard work, he built it into the most successful store in the chain. Walton cut costs by negotiating aggressively with his suppliers, and he kept the store open longer hours than his competition---tactics he brought with him when he struck out on his own and opened the first "Wal-Mart Discount City" in 1962.

Keep that in mind: Walton was 44 years old when he launched Wal-Mart. He'd spent more than a decade learning how to succeed in retail. He had insights into the business that his competitors didn't, and he put those advantages to work, full-bore.

Walton accomplished extraordinary things because of his insight, combined with his focus and drive. He routinely arrived at work at 4 a.m. As the company grew, he insisted on similar efforts from his people and gathered all of his senior managers for weekly Saturday morning meetings. He would steal away from family vacations to check out competitors' businesses. He'd motivate his employees by promising to do things like dance a hula in a grass skirt on Wall Street if the company met its earnings targets.

While Walton treated employees well in the long run---pay was decent while he headed the company and his associates shared in Wal-Mart's success---in the short run, he was very demanding. The typical image of a Wal-Mart executive became a harried, nervous businessman, scared to death of falling short of Walton's expectations. Even Walton's eventual successor as CEO was stricken with a heart attack at age 50 after an all-day meeting; everyone blamed the stress.

Still, Walton believed---correctly, as it turned out---that the members of his team needed him to set expectations high so that they could respond to them. He understood that his employees didn't need him to be their friend or their father. They needed him to be a truly assertive leader who could help them achieve greatness.

HIGH BETA VS. LOW BETA

Our advice diverges a bit from what some of the leading experts on business leadership and management might recommend, perhaps most typically the intellectual descendants of people like Peter F. Drucker and W. Edwards Deming. We want to reemphasize that the reason we offer differing advice is that we're talking about a small subset of organizations---high growth, dynamic entrepreneurial ventures. Most academics and experts, on the other hand, are trying to prescribe best practices for companies with larger scope and applicability. That means they're looking for predictable, repeatable, settled strategies. Oftentimes, they're willing to trade speed in favor of process and repeatability.

Put differently, they're looking for leadership styles that will lead to a lower *beta*---a lower-volatility, higher-predictability model, while we're advocating a different path for the small minority of businesses with founders like you, who hope to achieve fast, outsized growth. The traditional empowering leadership model will likely produce the most efficient use of capital and resources across an entire economy, but new ventures typically require a different, pragmatic approach.

Down the road, as your company grows, you'll rely much more on the Drucker and Deming empowering leadership models. Somewhere when you're going from the mid-hundreds of employees to the mid-thousands, you might have to bring in a Steve Balmer, as Bill Gates did at Microsoft, or an Eric Schmidt at Google. Even then, however, the most successful growing companies seem to benefit from having a strong, assertive leader as founder---someone who is passionate and knowledgeable, but who can hand off the structure and processes that are outside their strengths to people they trust.

That's later, though. When you're running a three-person company with a brand-new product in a brand-new market, how can you possibly know how to establish a bureaucracy? Why would you want to? You need to remain quick and nimble, ready to pursue opportunity wherever it might lead you.

ASSERTING VS. ENABLING

You might look at companies like Microsoft or Google and conclude that innovation can indeed survive within large bureaucracies. When many large technical companies roll out new products or innovations, though, these innovations are as likely as not to have had their genesis in smaller companies that the larger ones acquired. For example, in 2010, Google went on a buying spree, lapping up companies that had created innovations in social media. During one month alone, Google acquired six separate social networking companies for many millions of dollars. Think about this: for years, Google employed probably the most talented group of professional computer scientists assembled anywhere in the world. They had seemingly unlimited money, and they even told their employees to spend 20 percent of their time working on whatever they wanted to. With all that, who created the leading social network? A college kid in a dorm room---and now Google must go on a buying spree to have any hope of catching up.

Look at the Forbes list of the richest people in the world, and you'll see that almost everyone near the top of the list was either an assertive-leader-model entrepreneur, or else someone who inherited his or her wealth from such a person.

Kara Swisher, a former Wall Street Journal reporter who writes and produces the influential online publication AllThingsD, pays attention to these issues for a living. In many of today's most impressive entrepreneurial ventures, she told us, "there's one compelling entrepreneur at the center who calls all the shots ... You just have to have this compelling strong mind. Microsoft---[Bill Gates] had people working for him, but there was no question who was first among equals, if they were equals at all. There were no equals at Apple. There was Steve Jobs and there was everybody else. And sure it works. Why wouldn't it work?"

Here's another example. Today, Charles Ferguson is best known as the Academy Award-winning documentarian behind movies like *Inside Job*, about the financial crisis, and *No End in Sight*, about the American invasion of Iraq. In the mid-1990s, however, he was the CEO and founder of Vermeer Technologies, an early Internet software company. He had a strong vision, and he pushed his employees extremely hard. When the wife of one of his engineers had a baby, and the engineer took some time off to be with her, Ferguson reportedly called him at home and said he needed to get back in the office because he was not pulling his weight. The atmosphere got so tense that many employees wouldn't even speak to Ferguson anymore, so he had to have a second-in-command who could transmit his orders to the rest of the company.

Why was Ferguson so focused---an assertive leader to the point of seeming almost tyrannical? He had a sense that his company had only a small opportunity to grow and act. Vermeer Technologies developed software that allowed non-programmers to create web pages, a rarity at the time. Netscape was creating the first commercial browser, while Microsoft was working on Internet Explorer. It seemed obvious to Ferguson that one the two companies would start making software similar to his, which left him deathly afraid that the window of opportunity was going to close. He drove his team relentlessly for 100-hour weeks. The result was that his people performed, the company grew and they sold the whole thing to Microsoft for $133 million (which is why Ferguson is now able to spend his time directing documentaries). The product Ferguson's company made was renamed Microsoft FrontPage and integrated into its Office suite of programs.

It's useful to spend a few more minutes exploring what practicing these different approaches means in real life. Even for the motivated, assertive, perhaps somewhat egocentric founder, there will be moments of self-doubt---times when you're tempted to concede to the well-meaning advice of both external advisers and the smart, talented rock stars of their fields that you've recruited.

Think back to when we wrote about recruiting all of the knowledgeable, experienced people who specialize in different job functions, things like product engineering and sales. In the enabling-leader, process-oriented model, you'd train your team and make sure everyone's coordinated and working in sync. You'd develop a sophisticated, delegated management structure that divided responsibility and authority among different people. You'd describe objectives for each person and for the people that they work with, and ask for their help in setting up timelines and deliverables. You'd build processes to coordinate major decisions, create budgets and hold product planning meetings and marketing meetings. You'd have lots of training and activities to align people in terms of their understanding of the customer, the product, and their incentives.

But, the drawbacks quickly emerge. Things take longer, and the company becomes less innovative. You wind up with too many people weighing each decision. Individual contributors wind up thinking like individuals: *"I'm an HR specialist,"* or *"I'm an engineer,"* as opposed to, *"How do we come up with the useful innovations that we need in order to take the company forward?"* Your organization can quickly become rule-bound. As an entrepreneur, you simply don't have time for this. You might as well be back in the cubicle.

Instead, as an assertive-leader entrepreneur, you need to grow nearly obsessive when it comes to your vision, your focus, and your drive. You need to need to work long hours and get everyone to fall in line and support you. You often have to be determined to the point of obstinacy. You don't have time for lots of meetings and hand-wringing. Hopefully, this also means you'll have more internal consistency, because your business will be run by a single person as opposed to a committee. You'll make fewer design compromises and you'll probably get to market faster. Your product will likely be more coherent. If you're good, if you're the right person, you will probably come up with a better product than a committee could create.

We don't mean to downplay the side-effects. For example, Charles Ferguson says he was so stressed that he literally lost the ability to sleep for quite some time after he built Vermeer and sold it to Microsoft. Likewise, the assertive leader might run the risk of demoralizing members of his or her team who don't feel their contributions are being sufficiently listened to or respected. They probably joined at least in part because they had some degree of entrepreneurial spirit. But they may soon realize that they're going to be at best a bridesmaid in your company, never a bride---at least in the building stages. As the leader, you need to push hard, but try to do so without 100 percent alienating everyone. One strategy to achieve this that we'll explore in greater detail later is to plan many short-term wins. Be sure people know what goal they're working toward, so it doesn't seem they're in for endless toil without rewards.

Moreover, you might be concerned at times that you're wasting resources. Structure the organization so that you're making all the major decisions, and you might at times feel very alone. Once again, this is part of why it's so incredibly important to have done your homework and followed the framework as explained in the earlier modules of this book.

Finally, there's one more aspect to consider---a drawback to what we nevertheless feel is the most promising leadership style for an entrepreneur. They say success has a thousand fathers, but failure is an orphan. If things turn out well, then just about everyone involved will insist that he or she was a virtual cofounder and the real key to the company's success. You might not get all the credit you feel you deserve, but rest assured, you'll be blamed by everyone else in the company if things go wrong!

That's leadership. They say it's lonely at the top, but it's worse down below.

HOW TO LEAD AND MANAGE

Up until now we've been talking about leadership styles. As crucial as this is, of course, you also need to learn to employ *tactics* of leadership--- not just articulate what kind of leader you want to be. The best model we've found for leading a small, dynamic group under the assertive leadership model is the eight-step framework that Professor John Kotter advocates. (In fact, this is the model that the coauthor of this book, Jon Burgstone, used as the CEO and co-founder of his company, SupplierMarket, which he and his cofounder built and sold for $1.1 billion---in a single year.)

CREATE URGENCY

Good work requires attention and focus. Whether you're working on a project, trying to close a negotiation, or making sales, smart entrepreneurs create deadlines that can spur people to action. Think about it. College students pull all-nighters and write papers at the last minute. Legislatures debate for months and then pass a budget when there's almost no time left in the session. Psychologists hear the most important bits of insight from patients at the end of the session---the so-called "doorknob confession." This common phenomenon can drive you crazy as an entrepreneur, but you can also harness the power of urgency to your advantage.

Here's how this worked at SupplierMarket. The company launched in the summer of 1999, and Burgstone asked his engineers for the earliest date on which they could promise the Internet application would be up and running. Their answer was October 18. With that in mind, Burgstone arranged to have 50,000 letters mailed out to potential customers on October 15. Of course, as the date approached, some of the engineers grew nervous, suggesting they wouldn't make October 18 after all. But by then, the letters had been processed and sent to the distribution facility, and there was no way to stop them.

The end result? The engineers pulled together, worked incredibly hard, and successfully launched the site on October 18 at 6 a.m. They quite likely cursed Burgstone every hour but they put in heroic efforts and got it done. It was a good thing, too. The 50,000 letters prompted so much traffic that SupplierMarket's servers overloaded and eventually crashed on the first day. If you're going to have problems as an entrepreneur, those are the kind you don't mind having.

FORM A POWERFUL COALITION

It can be daunting to launch a new initiative or venture on your own, so you want to recruit others to stand out there with you.

It helps you build credibility, but it also leaves the people you've recruited wanting you to succeed.

Now, expand your constellation of stakeholders. Get people involved who are decision-makers elsewhere, who can impact your business with a "thumbs up" or a "thumbs down." Convince them to associate themselves with you, make introductions, or vouch for you.

Every time you send out a newsletter or do an interview now, you want to think of a way to give credit to a member of your board of advisors or to an investor, or someone else on your team. You're praising and thanking them, but you're also holding them accountable. Tell the world that they're part of this group designing a product that's going to launch by a certain date, because then they'll be publicly on the hook for it.

CREATE A VISION FOR CHANGE

With urgency and a powerful group of people behind you, this is the step where you really get to stand up and lead. You probably have a good sense of your vision already, but think hard about how you want to communicate it to your stakeholders. Sales comes down to two things: offering the most compelling promise you can possibly make, consistent with your ability to deliver. Think back to the customer pain you're solving, and your value proposition. (*People want clean teeth*, or else, *People want teeth*.) Your team wants to believe in you, and to feel that you're leading them somewhere worth their time and effort. Listen to your customers. Listen to your stakeholders and the members of that powerful coalition you're building. Refine the vision, sure, but at the end of the day, articulate it---loudly, clearly, and passionately.

Here are a couple of real-life examples---and you'll notice that they're similar to the process of identifying the customer pain that each venture is set up to solve. Think of Apple: Is the company's vision to build personal computers? Or is it to *simplify the most advanced technology for everyone?* Wal-Mart? *Bring inexpensive goods to everyone.* Toyota? *Make the world's most dependable automobiles.* Google? *Organize the world's information.* Robin Chase wanted to *make car use more efficient.*

You don't have to want to launch the next Google in order to follow this advice, but it helps to express your vision this way. Just be creative, enthusiastic, and real. The cupcake entrepreneur in Omaha doesn't simply want to sell baked goods. He or she wants to *bring people pleasure, one bite at a time.*

COMMUNICATE YOUR VISION

You want people within your organization to use similar language to describe what you're trying to do. Note that this isn't the old politician's media trick of sticking to sound bites and answering the question you wish you were asked no matter what the questioner wants to know, so much as a matter of getting your team to understand and communicate similarly at a core level.

One important part of creating that kind of culture is to ensure that you communicate with your team regularly about the big picture. You don't want the techie focusing exclusively on the product or the salesperson focusing exclusively on numbers. You want to ensure that they pay attention to how their individual efforts contribute to the overall goals. So find a way to borrow from Sam Walton and his Saturday morning meetings. Get your team together regularly. One successful entrepreneur we know decided that Saturday mornings are too much to ask, but he brings together his entire 300-person team for a one-hour, big-picture meeting every Thursday afternoon. Make sure everyone steps back from the day-to-day challenges and focuses on the long-term vision. You'll likely find it's a lot easier to get them to buy into that vision when they understand it.

REMOVE OBSTACLES

You've been removing obstacles since the very first pages of this book, when we talked about finding business ideas with the least business and technical risk. Focus on these areas now with specificity. Ask your team members what they need to be more efficient and insist that they come up with innovative ways to reduce both business and technical risk. Pay attention to qualitative metrics---hard data---and continually improve your development, manufacturing, and distribution processes.

Be constantly on the lookout for the great things your team members achieve. When they find ways to improve your product or get it to market more efficiently, praise them the best way possible: by publicly acknowledging their innovations and implementing those innovations in your plan going forward.

CREATE SHORT-TERM WINS

Plan early successes. As you map out the steps you need to take to achieve your goals, make sure that you include intermediate milestones so you have something to celebrate when you achieve them. This will motivate your team, generate confidence and promote your external credibility. It also helps your relationships with stakeholders, because when you ask them for more resources, you can point to your tangible, measurable achievements.

Think of things that report legitimate progress, but that you can also control. Maybe it's celebrating when you create a prototype and start sharing it with potential customers. Regardless of whether their feedback is positive or negative, it's still a win, because you're learning something new about your market that can lead to additional unique insights.

Team members want to feel that they're a part of something successful. They want to be able to tell their friends and families,

"We hit a big milestone this week," and that they contributed to it. Moreover, you're going to have to deal with some hurt feelings and resentment at times if you follow the assertive leadership model, but people will be willing to put up with a lot more on a daily basis if they can take pride in what they've accomplished after weeks or months.

BUILD ON CHANGE

Never rest on your laurels. After you've spent an hour or an evening celebrating your small wins, immediately reassess how much more you are now able to accomplish as a result. By achieving small victories, you've changed the playing field a bit. You know more, and you're known better. This is the time to heighten your ambitions and seize the momentum.

We're almost back to the first step in the Kotter process again: creating urgency. What you want do now is consider how much higher you can set your sights. Determine what intermediate steps are needed to get there---and, once again set out to foster the need to achieve specific things by specific deadlines.

ANCHOR CHANGES IN CORPORATE CULTURE

This final step helps you maintain your momentum. You want to create a culture that values the traits and accomplishments you need and recognizes people when they exemplify them. Would Wal-Mart's market position tumble into a freefall if its executives started getting their own rooms at Motel 6? Probably not, but nearly two decades after Sam Walton's death, the company's culture still has keeping costs low at its core.

Just as you hold the people who fall short accountable, hold up those who accomplish great things as examples. Communicate how valuable you think they are. Get in the habit of recording your history and creating some mythology about your company. You can get caught up easily in the day-to-day, so it's motivating to have a long-term record of just how much you've accomplished.

You'll also find this is valuable when you recruit new team members. They weren't there to live through the early times, but you want to instill in them the same excitement and values. Especially once you grow past a dozen or 20 team members, you'll want to have some kind of efficient way to communicate your values to the newcomers.   Having written materials, presentations, or even just a truthful but well-practiced story of how you got to where you are can help you communicate your passion effectively.

THE BIG PICTURE

The life of an assertive leader can take its toll on an entrepreneur, and it can also be hard to pull off. If you're going to pursue this strategy---and it probably offers you the greatest chances of success for an early-stage, high-growth venture---then you can see why once again the concepts in the rest of this book (especially the first several modules) are so important. If you haven't developed a truly compelling business idea that solves true customer pain, offers a compelling value proposition, and reaches a large enough market, then where's the use in insisting that others work hard to achieve your vision? Unfortunately, you can probably point to many companies (perhaps even some where you've worked) where the leadership follows some variation of the assertive style but the core business underlying everything simply doesn't make sense.

However, if you have truly answered the questions at the start of this book and have developed a compelling, problem-solving business, take confidence from that fact and act accordingly. Will some of your team members push back at times? Almost certainly, but in the end the results will speak for themselves. Not everyone at Apple loved Steve Jobs, but the company has accomplished amazing feats.

You're the one who came up with the vision, the one who articulated it and tested it, and who has assembled the resources. You're the one who went out and gathered the unique information that gives you an advantage in the market.

Remember, your team isn't looking for nurturing and excuses. They're looking for a leader, and that means they're looking to you. So, pursue the opportunity, and be the man or woman who assertively leads your new venture to greatness.

MODULE 9

"I think of ventures as roller coasters, not rocket ships."

- Professor Bill Sahlman,

Harvard Business School

"If you don't like the thrill of a roller coaster, if you're not willing to get thrown around, don't get on the roller coaster."

- Dean Kamen,

Segway inventor

MAINTAINING BALANCE AND LIVING THE ENTREPRENEURIAL LIFE

No matter how successful you may ultimately become, we can make an ironclad prediction: There will be moments in your entrepreneurial journey when you'll wonder what on earth you were thinking by choosing this path. New ventures are all-consuming. While they're often exciting, it's not always exciting in a good way!

There are things you can do, however, to make the entrepreneurial road more balanced and enjoyable. You can start a company that fits your values. You can start a company first and foremost because you want to start a company---not because you hope to get rich.

You'll have your moments, though. How do the most successful entrepreneurs get through them?

The biggest employer of new graduates at many top U.S. colleges and universities today---Yale, Dartmouth, Duke, and Georgetown among them---isn't a consulting firm, a Fortune 500 company, or a government agency. It's Teach For America, the program that recruits promising young people and convinces them to work in the most under-resourced schools in the country.

Founded by Wendy Kopp, TFA has its roots in her Princeton undergraduate thesis, "A Plan and Argument for the Creation of a National Teacher Corps." As a young social entrepreneur just starting out, she scrounged resources like a champion. She convinced the CEO of Union Carbide to provide her with free office space in Manhattan. She cajoled donors for initial grants and hired an administrative staff. Her team recruited thousands of applicants, and they convinced urban school chiefs and principals to hire their teachers ("corps members," in TFA parlance).

Then came the first fall. A respected school superintendent left Kopp in tears by telling her that the last thing he needed was a bunch of Ivy League do-gooders meddling in his district. A city-wide teachers' strike in New Orleans left TFA wondering whether to tell its corps members to cross the picket lines or pay them out of its tight budget. Elsewhere, a handful of its corps members were laid off in Los Angeles and New York City due to budget cuts and "last in, first out" provisions. Then, the schools where some other TFA corps members were supposed to teach closed.

Just as often, miracles would appear almost out of nowhere. TFA faced a $2.5 million annual shortfall, and Kopp's solution was to fly to Texas and ask billionaire Ross Perot---whom she'd never met and had no real connection to---to make up the difference. Incredibly, it worked. Later, they were short of funds again and within pennies of missing payroll. A funder whose company had pledged $250,000 spontaneously increased the donation to $350,000 without being asked.

Still, Kopp had never led anything like this effort before. She often felt completely overwhelmed. She found she didn't like public speaking, a key skill for someone in her position. Her staff revolted at times. One meeting of key leaders spiraled so far out of control that it was later referred to in corps lore as "the night of a thousand suggestions." Meantime, Kopp faced the unexpected temptation of lucrative job offers. "It seems something of a miracle that I maintained my confidence throughout that first year," Kopp later wrote. "Why didn't I crumble under the stress or the workload? Why didn't I despair?"

That's a key question for just about any entrepreneur to ask ahead of time. When the going gets tough, what will keep you going?

THE PERSONAL NATURE OF STARTUPS

Win or lose, the entrepreneurial life is one of ups and downs. The good news for entrepreneurs is that over time, if you remain smart and focused, you will almost certainly experience much higher highs than the ones you would have if you'd chosen a more traditional career. Of course, it's almost never a straight shot to the top. One day you will climb high, the next you will fall low. It will happen over and over again, in swings much greater than non-entrepreneurs experience.

We're evangelists for entrepreneurship, but we recognize that aversion to pain and fear of short-term lows can be good reasons not to pursue this path. People can legitimately value stability. They can certainly contribute to the world, and live meaningful lives. If we hear one thing over and over again from hugely successful entrepreneurs, it's that there is no way to avoid the highs and lows of this life if you choose it.

So, how do you manage life while starting a company? How do you maintain your sanity and have healthy relationships with the people you care about, if you feel like you're alternating between professionally living, dying and being reborn, day after day?

Let's go back to our opening example. Why didn't Wendy Kopp crumble under the stress? What was it that enabled her to weather the unending cycle of ups and downs? In a phrase, it was that she believed so strongly in what she was doing.

There is a trip Kopp talks about taking in the first or second year of TFA. She and a colleague flew to Los Angeles, where they visited Compton High School---a dark, depressing building with peeling paint in a rough neighborhood. Later, she headed to dinner with a group of politicians and donors and wound up staying overnight with one donor's family in Bel-Air. She "woke up to a gorgeous view of a glistening swimming pool and sun-strewn tennis court," Kopp later recalled. She couldn't stop thinking about the contrasts between two worlds she'd visited.

Constantly being reminded of that kind of disparity, the bright shining line between haves and have-nots, kept Kopp motivated. It seems clear that TFA was aligned almost perfectly with her personal values and goals. Kopp pushed forward with aggressive expansion plans even when many of her staff and her mentors urged caution. She drew CEOs like Steve Jobs and politicians like Hillary Clinton to the cause. She kept traveling---25 trips across the country in her second year alone---raising money, recruiting, and evangelizing.

The result is that today, Teach for America corps members have taught 3 million students in 43 regions around the country. The roughly 20,000 TFA alumni are now a force in education and politics. How did Kopp get there?

"It was a blind faith," she later wrote, "in the power of the idea."

THREE APPROACHES

Most entrepreneurs start more than one venture in their lifetimes. Almost all have other demands on their time as well. They have families and friends, hobbies and interests, spiritual and charitable pursuits. How do they manage it all? Over the years, the entrepreneurs we've interviewed have employed many different strategies, but three really stand out: the *dedication/obsession* approach, the *holistic/ spiritual* approach, and the *engineered-happiness* approach.

There are some commonalities among the three. Perhaps the most important is the idea that people are happiest when they use their natural abilities meaningfully and to their fullest potential.

THE DEDICATED/OBSESSIVE APPROACH

Some people are fortunate enough not simply to be athletes, musicians, or scientists, but to be programmed so that they'll truly enjoy those kinds of pursuits. They're "naturals." While we come down clearly on the side of nurture over nature when it comes to how entrepreneurs develop their abilities, it's also clear that some people are predisposed to become entrepreneurs. They're simply so hard-wired to be entrepreneurs. They're simply so hard-wired to enjoy the entrepreneurial struggle that they likely won't be able to function well in any other environment.

Even if this doesn't sound like you, it's a good idea to try to understand the mindset. Chances are it will describe some of your competitors.

BUSINESS EXAMPLE:

NEARLY COMPLETE OBSESSION

Darian Shirazi was a high school senior when he first met Sean Parker, founder of Napster and Plaxo. Soon, Parker recruited Darian to a programming internship at a new startup he was working with: "the facebook."

Even in a company started by Harvard dropouts and 20-somethings, Darian stood out for his youth. He loved the atmosphere. As great an experience as it was, however, many of the others who had been to college suggested that Darian ought to at least give higher education a try. It wasn't certain whether Facebook would be a great success in 2006, so Darian took their advice. He left Facebook and enrolled at the University of California, Berkeley.

Later, he considered this a tremendous mistake.

"I was in this cookie cutter environment," he said. "We have a society so focused on that kind of performance and getting good grades. I just considered that hell. I realized I have no desire to do this."

The one thing that did excite him was the idea of starting something new. Darian and some classmates eventually launched a company called

Redux that would allow users to tag photos of people they found attractive and find similar-looking people on Internet dating sites. They left school, raised money, worked hard---and it all quickly fell apart.

It hurt. "I was kicked out," Darian said. "Kicked out as CEO by the cofounder and investors. I went through a bad time. I was like, 'We all really messed up.'"

When he considered what he'd done wrong, Darian decided he hadn't been sufficiently committed. He hadn't lived and breathed Redux 24/7, and as a result, he hadn't understood everything he could about the market he was in. Next time, he wouldn't make that mistake.

He and another Berkeley classmate teamed up on a new venture, and this time their commitment was total. They moved into Darian's parents' house for five months to start Fwix, a hyperlocal, geo-targeted content site. Eventually, they moved into a house of their own and brought on two other employees to live and work with them. Four young guys, sleeping four hours a night, packed two-to-a-bedroom at 314 Poe Street in Palo Alto---it was kind of like the atmosphere he'd experienced in the early days at Facebook.

"You should have seen how we had it set up," Darian recalled. "It was the perfect house to start a company. We slept literally feet from each other. It was like the battlefield, or a bunker as we liked to call it. We would walk down every morning to Palo Alto to get breakfast, talking about the product 24/7. We were breathing more of the product than we breathed air."

Great. Is this the new standard? Move in with your cofounders so you can commit everything to the business, 24/7?

For some people, maybe. It's still too early to pronounce Fwix a success, but the company got funded, grew, and did more than a million dollars in revenue in its second year. Darian says the difference this time has been his near-obsessive commitment.

"It was to the point where I said, I am not going to go out and meet new people. I'm not going to meet friends except holidays," he told us. "You can't have another life. You're so focused on the problem. *How can I get it to work? How can I get customers and users?* If you are really in it and passionate about it, you won't want another life."

That said, few can keep up that pace forever. After two years, Darian eased back a bit, hired a few more people, and delegated more. The company got gym memberships for everyone, and they looked at renting a place in Tahoe so they'd have somewhere to go and relax. That said, the money means almost nothing to him. In fact, based on his tenure at Facebook as an 18-year-old, Darian probably never really needs to work again, at least not for financial reasons.

Still, he added, "I'm living and breathing it as much as I can right now." They've outgrown the Palo Alto house, but he lives a block away from Fwix's San Francisco office.

"I don't think you can teach this," he said. "I see things that entrepreneurs have in common, like a burning desire to build something. They're not happy when they're taking instruction or direction from somewhere else."

THE HOLISTIC/SPIRITUAL APPROACH

Can entrepreneurship intrinsically bring fulfillment? Some entrepreneurs seem to believe so. In their worlds, the process of creative destruction itself, with its focus on constant revolution and problem solving, is what leads people to higher levels of consciousness and truer truths. They find it especially fulfilling to fuel the journey based on their personal strengths.

NOT-QUITE-A-BUSINESS EXAMPLE:
A RELIGIOUS ENTREPRENEUR

An Episcopal clergyman named William Swing started his career more than a half-century ago at a makeshift church in rural West Virginia with just 20 parishioners, meeting every Sunday in a former plumber's workshop in the shadow of a steel mill. It was part of his job to build ties within the community, so he recruited the steel mill's president as a parishioner. The congregation grew quickly, the parish expanded, and within a few years, Swing was presiding over four separate churches. Sundays were busy.

A few years later, Swing got a new assignment: Washington, DC. During his decade there, he grew his new church from 300 parishioners to 2,500, adding worship services geared toward families with small children. He got the idea of having parishioners write and produce a full-length, Broadway-style musical on the life of the church's patron saint. It was a huge success. The cast traveled the world to perform. One of the singers, Karen Allen, went on to become a successful Hollywood actress and the female lead in "Raiders of the Lost Ark."

Swing's next home was California, where he became a bishop. He opened a church shelter when the homeless crisis first began and wound up housing 1,000 to 1,500 people every night for 25 years. He reached out to the gay community in San Francisco. In the wake of the Rodney King riots in Los Angeles, he helped launch a community development bank to rebuild. The church got involved with a nonprofit hospital in dire straits. When finances grew especially tight, Swing golfed with the CEO of another hospital, and convinced him over 18 holes to help save it.

Not long before his 70th birthday, Swing got the idea to start an international organization of religions, modeled after the United Nations. He traveled the world trying to convince religious leaders to send representatives to join the interfaith group, but he found very few takers. Door after door closed in his face. When he gave a speech promoting the idea at Oxford University, he was booed off the stage.

Swing was nearing retirement. He wondered if it was time to take a few years off---to relax a bit, if not flat-out retire for good. He'd built some fantastic things, and he and his wife had raised two children. He'd traveled the world. Heck, he was an avid golfer with a 9-handicap.

Still, he couldn't quite shake the feeling that he had at least one major struggle left to undertake. How could he leave this new idea of an organization of world religions alone? Did he have the talents and temperament needed to make it happen?

It might seem a bit odd to be talking about an Episcopal bishop in a book about entrepreneurship. Frankly Swing felt that way, too when we first talked to him.

He had never considered the definition of the word entrepreneurship, or even quite figured out how to spell it, until he was in his seventh decade. He didn't consider himself a great theologian. But when he thought about the things that had made him successful in life, he acknowledged they were entrepreneurial traits. He took joy in the idea of building things out of nothing---or, perhaps more accurately, arranging people and resources so that they could build things they'd never dreamed of individually. From his first church in West Virginia, that was what he'd done, naturally.

As he neared retirement, Swing decided to keep moving forward on his idea for an organization of world religions. The group he founded, the United Religions Initiative, would seek to bring together adherents of different faiths into groups called cooperation circles. He wound up signing personally for $1 million in credit in order to fund the effort. Instead of living off a nest egg and enjoying a life of retirement, he and his wife instead stared at an immense new challenge---while deeply in debt.

In fact, the whole thing seemed almost impossible at times. How could you organize people from various faiths and get them to work together, especially when many of the religions viewed each other as heretical, or worse?

"The impossibility of the task is the thing that makes it so attractive," Swing said. "The joy of being an entrepreneur is the hunt, the chase. It's almost an elaborate game. There's something utterly enticing, because backing down isn't an option."

The United Religions Initiative now has almost 2.5 million people involved. As a religious man, Swing thinks of his work as a search for the will of God, but this might be applicable no matter whether you believe in religion, or the universe, or any higher or greater force you can imagine.

"Entrepreneurs," Swing told us, "are always on a pilgrimage which finally leads to the realm of the Spirit, the Creator and the Creation. Inexorably, one has to end up in the field of 'the ultimate.'"

The Engineered-Happiness Approach

Most entrepreneurs probably have many needs that they have to fill in order to feel whole. They have families to care for, they feel spiritual callings; they simply have hobbies or less serious interests. The engineered happiness approach suggests that there are fundamental strengths and virtues that can be empirically shown to lead to a fuller happiness. They also happen to overlap greatly with the attributes that might make people more successful entrepreneurs. The question adherents to this approach usually wind up asking is a classic one: Can you have it all?

BUSINESS EXAMPLE:
WHICH DO YOU DO FIRST?

Drew Griffin looked around the table. He saw himself in the faces of the eight university students that he and two others from his group, the Young Presidents Organization, had taken to dinner.

He remembered being their age, considering career options but knowing deep inside that he'd never truly be happy working for someone else. He'd spent three years at a large company before launching his venture at age 28. By 32, Griffin had 65 employees, and was doing more than $10 million a year in revenue, milestones that had made him eligible for membership in the YPO.

He'd worked hard over the decade that followed and the business had done well. He'd recently calculated that he'd spent more than 32,000 hours at work over that time, an average of something like 65 hours a week, every week. But it had paid off. Now, he'd been looking forward to this evening ever since the chapter president had asked him to come. It felt like a stamp of approval, a valedictory, and he was glad for the chance to share what he'd learned.

The students' questions, however, surprised him. They initially wanted to learn about his business model and how he'd gathered the courage to leave his safe corporate job to begin with. But then conversation quickly turned to work-life balance.

"Are you married?" one of the students asked. "How does working so much affect that relationship?"

"What are your passions outside of work?" another wanted to know. "Are you 'happy'?"

"You're thinking about this all wrong," Griffin said after a moment. "You should think about work-life balance over the course of a lifetime, not over the course of a day or a week."

"Exactly," another YPO member at the table chimed in. "If you want a strategy, the one that worked for me was to work very hard at a young age, and then later to focus on the other aspects of my life."

The third YPO member spoke up as well. Sure, he had passions, but the top priority had to be his business.

"People get on a career trajectory by the time they're in their late 20s or early 30s. By the time you're 35 or 40, you know who you're going to be. It's very hard to make a drastic change after that."

The university students' body language suggested they disagreed. They seemed to want to hear that they could have it all.

"I have a family," Griffin said, breaking the awkward silence.

"But my twins are barely two years old," he continued. "They're not going to remember being age two. When they turn five, that's the time to think about throttling back on work a bit to start spending more time with my family. You don't get the option to do that, though, unless you've worked hard and made sacrifices ahead of time."

Consciously or not, most entrepreneurs take sides in a fundamental debate about how to manage their lives in the context of building a great business. That question is: Should you address your growth in other life dimensions (things like spiritual development, physical health, and love and relationships) at the same time that you grow your business and professional career? Is the smarter strategy to devote time and energy to all four of these dimensions sequentially?

We don't necessarily endorse the sequential strategy that Drew Griffin and the YPO members described, but it's important that you understand how some of the competition thinks. Is it really possible to put virtually all of your effort into your professional life for years, only to suddenly switch gears and change priorities at age 35 or

40? We're not entirely convinced. Even for those who achieve their professional goals, the difficulty is that if you make $10 million, then you'll likely be in a position to meet people and see what life is like for those with $100 million. It can be very hard to stop.

OVERCOMING CONSUMERISM

Dr. Martin Seligman, a professor of psychology at the University of Pennsylvania and former president of the American Psychological Association, is one of the true authorities on engineering happiness. One of the real impediments people face, his research suggests, is what he calls the "hedonic treadmill." People work to earn more money, so that they can buy more things, and feel short-term blips of pleasure or contentment. But then they adapt quickly to their new circumstances.

People may think they want to be rich, but usually what they really want is the freedom and the lifestyle that they think being rich will provide them. Real income in the United States rose about 16 percent in the 30 years before Seligman wrote the book, *Authentic Happiness*, but the percentage of people who described themselves as "very happy" fell from 36 percent to 29 percent over the same period.

Certainly we don't mean to glorify poverty, but the truth is that once you reach a certain fairly comfortable level of income---studies show it's generally not much more than $75,000--- more money doesn't add to happiness. At that level in America, you're comfortably middle-class. Living in most parts of the country, you can afford decent housing, food, medical coverage, and transportation. Past that, we're just talking about whether you drive a Lexus or a Toyota.

There are a lot of paths that a smart, educated person can follow in America to reach $75,000 a year, in a fairly short period of time. If that's truly the threshold past which more money doesn't buy happiness, then to what degree should acquiring additional income govern your career and professional choices?

Back to our fundamental questions: What kept Wendy Kopp going in the darkest times at TFA? Why did Bishop Swing cast aside his retirement---the relaxing "golden years" we're told most Americans spend their lives looking forward to---in order to start United Religions? What prompted Darian Shirazi to drop out of school and work extreme hours to start a new company when he'd already made enough money to never have to work again?

One of the keys is that doing so aligned closely with their personal values. So why doesn't everyone do that?

The problem is that most of us are influenced by so many outside forces that impact what we *think our values should be* rather than what we're really comfortable with and care a lot about. Parents, teachers, peers, and our society at large impact us greatly. How do you really know that your values belong to you and are not simply the reflection of those around you? How can you be happy and live a full life without deeply understanding your unique personal values?

Unfortunately, this seems to be the norm. Why do so many people in their early and mid-twenties study law, medicine, engineering, or business---fields that they likely know very little about when they make the initial time and financial commitments? They often make their choices to please other people; in other words, based on other peoples' values. A few years later, a lot of lawyers, doctors, engineers, or other professionals conclude that if they'd truly chosen a path based on what they valued, they would have picked something completely different. Next thing you know, you have doctors announcing that what they really wanted to do was study cooking, lawyers moonlighting as standup comedians, and MBAs leaving corporate positions to work for nonprofits.

Beyond the question of happiness, it can be very hard to succeed professionally in a career that doesn't match your values. Suppose a fairly laid-back person who values a friendly, social atmosphere succumbs to someone else's values---parents, a professor---and goes to law school. A few years later, she winds up working in a competitive, adversarial law firm. Either she tries to adjust her personality and values to fit the professional culture, or else she "fails" in her career. If she tries to act like two different people depending on what time of day it is and where she's sitting, she's likely to grow highly dissatisfied.

Over time, it's rare and probably unhealthy that people can separate what they do for ten or twelve hours a day at work with how they behave for four hours at night when they get home.

The lesson seems to be to ask yourself early and often: What are my strengths in life? What do I want to do? How do I know?

THE BIG PICTURE

You've no doubt noticed that most of the highly successful entrepreneurs we've interviewed did not cite the desire to make a lot of money as their primary motivation. Don't get us wrong. Money is important. But if it's your sole motivator in becoming an entrepreneur, you're probably not going to find contentment and happiness in this life.

As important as your new venture is, man cannot live on startups alone. Top entrepreneurs we've talked with cite service to others, the development of family and loving relationships, paying attention to your physical health, and committing yourself to lifelong learning as keys to happiness and success. Keep them in mind throughout your journey. The habits and priorities you establish in the early days of your new venture are likely to have an impact on how you live your life once you achieve great success with it.

Just as entrepreneurs need to find true customer pain and understand value propositions before they launch their ventures, they also need to ask themselves ahead of time what they really believe, and what will really make them happy and fulfilled. The best sort of entrepreneurship is not about the pursuit of cash, fame, or accolades. Using your strengths to contribute to the world is what brings true gratification. Embrace the lifestyle, because the effect of your success as an entrepreneur can be the kind of creative destruction that a society needs in order to progress.

MODULE 10

"The reasonable man adapts himself to the world; the unreasonable man persists in trying to adapt the world to himself. Therefore all progress depends on the unreasonable man."

- George Bernard Shaw

LEARNING TO EXPECT AND ACHIEVE MORE

You've studied the framework. You now know how to brainstorm, test ideas, gather resources, build credibility, lead, and manage. You've explored the economic forces that weigh heavily in your favor when you launch a truly promising venture. You have the strategy you need to succeed.

If past experience is a guide, however, many of us will never actually try to get a new venture off the ground. What holds us back? Why don't we strive for and achieve greatness? Most importantly, how will you buck the trend?

We've mentioned a few times the experiences of coauthor Jon Burgstone, whose first entrepreneurial success came after he teamed up with a business school classmate named Asif Satchu. Together, Jon and Asif started a company that they called SupplierMarket, which became the first Internet marketplace for custom-made manufactured parts. Neither Jon nor Asif came from great wealth. They weren't the sons of world-class entrepreneurs. They had no greater advantages than most of their peers. So how did they convince themselves that they deserved to achieve outsized success?

The answer is that they consciously developed great (and perhaps even absurdly unrealistic) expectations of themselves and those around them. There is one moment in particular that Jon talks about when he had to reinforce his expanded expectations to fill the field he was playing on. Just a few months into their venture, he and Asif had the chance to seek investment from Sequoia Capital, a renowned firm that had previously invested in companies including Atari, Apple, Cisco Systems, Electronic Arts and Oracle. While Jon and Asif had celebrated many short-term wins in their company's short history, pitching Sequoia meant they were suddenly thrust into a big game in the major leagues.

Jon and Asif sat scanning the conference room as they waited for the investor meeting to begin. The meeting table was old and chipped. The walls were decorated with free posters bearing the logos of the firm's biggest successes. The decor reinforced Jon's understanding that Sequoia didn't invest in things that didn't promise a return. He wondered about the source of the vaguely musty odor he smelled.

Suddenly it hit him: The beat-up old chairs they were sitting in? They were likely the same ones Steve Jobs and Steve Wozniak sat in when they first came to Sequoia. The 1970s-era table? It might well have been the one where Larry Ellison sat when he came to raise money for Oracle.

Jon's heart raced faster. He felt pangs of doubt. Who did he think he was? He was just eighteen months removed from being a twenty-something engineer at Ford. Their company was still an unproven idea. He and Asif hadn't paid themselves a penny in salary. There wasn't even a website yet at suppliermarket.com.

Jon heard the voice of reason in the back of his mind: *"What gives you the right even to aspire to this?"*

He and Asif exchanged silent looks. Did they really think they were going to follow in the footsteps of people like Jobs and Ellison? Jon's palms sweated. He heard the firm's partners approaching in the hallway.

WHAT MAKES IT SO HARD TO BELIEVE?

An entrepreneur needs to solve customer pain, offer a compelling value proposition, sell, build, lead, and pursue a balanced life---but he also has to believe. He has to embrace the attitude of entrepreneurial inevitability that we explained back at the start of this journey.

For all our talk about creative destruction, entrepreneurship often doesn't intuitively feel sensible on an individual level. Setting out on your own is the exact opposite of what most people will advise you to do. It's not reasonable to think that you can do what most don't. And yet without smart, ambitious, unreasonable people who are willing to take those leaps, society sees little progress.

At the end of the day, you either jump or you don't. That said, there are at least four things that you can do to make it easier to learn to have faith.

First, *train yourself to expect outsized outcomes.* An entrepreneur must be at least somewhat subversive. He must train himself to believe that he is entitled to greatness. It's ironic. Just about every human being who has ever walked the planet had the potential to achieve great outcomes, but most never do so. Why? Because they don't believe they can. Those who do demand more, who expect greatness, who exhibit audacity---coupled with genuine insights and systematic planning---win. It's always the outsider. It's always the entrepreneur.

Second, *learn to manage your fear.* Fear holds us back, but most often we're afraid of things that don't make logical sense. So again, you have to train yourself to overcome them. Modern psychology teaches that the most effective way to overcome trepidation is to expose yourself gradually to the object of your dread. If fears are irrational, exposing them carefully for what they are can make them less potent.

Third, *find external validation.* Most of your drive as an entrepreneur has to come from inside, but you can't do it alone. It doesn't take much sometimes---just a few early customer orders or sincere encouragement from people whose opinions you respect can add steel to your spine. So, take steps ahead of time so you'll know these kinds of people when their vote of confidence can make the difference.

Finally, *follow the framework.* We want you to believe---but only in things that are real. Everything in *Breakthrough Entrepreneurship* is intended to teach you how to reject a thousand marginal ideas in favor of the best ones, and then maximize your chances of success with them. Testing and obtaining maximum information for minimum cost is an absolute prerequisite to developing faith in your new venture.

ENGINEERING EXPECTATIONS

Let's pick up with Jon and Asif. As entrepreneurs, they employed all of the practical strategies we've talked about in this book. Jon overcame his moment of self-doubt in the Sequoia conference room and the firm invested. He and Asif built SupplierMarket into an industry leader that created hundreds of jobs and offered a revolutionary new way for manufacturers to do business with each other---a market that lives on today. They sold the whole thing for more than a billion dollars, and they did it all within a single year. Their entrepreneurial adventures were so textbook perfect that they became the subject of two separate Harvard Business School case studies on how to start amazing new companies.

Both Jon and Asif went on to be successful as investors and in other entrepreneurial endeavors. Jon started the Center for Entrepreneurship at the University of California, Berkeley. Since he turned to teaching, hundreds of his students have followed in his footsteps and started companies of their own. Many have made millions. He has also started and currently manages a very successful private investment partnership. Meanwhile, Asif went on to start two other successful companies in completely different industries. He was the cofounder of one of the largest self-storage companies in Canada, and then cofounded Media Rights Capital, the largest independent film financing company in Hollywood.

Sitting high above Los Angeles, in the spacious, glass-walled headquarters of Asif's latest venture, it would be easy to assume that he and Jon have always lived lives like this. But the truth is that you have to look deep into their pasts and their characters to figure out what it was that set them apart.

Jon grew up in a middle class family in suburban Chicago, the son of an oil refinery worker. Remember Hansen Enterprises from Module 3, the firm that developed the technology for Roller Blades, but never targeted a vast market or made much money? That was Jon's grandfather's company. Asif came from even humbler beginnings. Born in Kenya, he immigrated with his parents first to England and then Canada before finally coming to the U.S. for work and education. He remembers his family sharing a two-bedroom apartment with another family when they first arrived, and being picked on and beaten up as a kid in grade school.

As we neared the end of writing this book, we brought them together to answer some important questions. What set them apart? Why is it that they have been able to start and build great ventures over and over again---while so many others haven't?

EXPECTING OUTSIZED OUTCOMES

Managing fear helps cut some of the ties that pull us back, but equally important is strengthening the muscles that push us forward. You don't just want to minimize or manage your fear; you want to build within yourself an expectation of success.

Jon and Asif were both quite young when they started SupplierMarket, but they already had a record of exceeding their previous successes with each new venture. They'd both worked in several serious jobs each---as an automotive engineer, a banker and a business consultant, for example.

"Are you familiar with the Pygmalion effect?" asked Jon, referring to the theory that says the higher the expectations you place on people, the better they will perform. "My experiences made me feel like I could figure just about anything out. At the end of the day, you just figure out the steps and then do it. Few jobs in modern life are really that difficult to understand, at least compared to mastering differential equations [which he had studied as a college engineering major]."

Asif cited another factor: He grew up watching his father's experience. Over time his father enjoyed significant business success, but his parents shielded Asif from seeing the inevitable lows along the way.

"My dad initially struggled for the first couple years ... but I had no idea," Asif recalled. It wasn't until years later, when he read a newspaper article about his father, that he learned how close he'd come to calling it quits and taking a job as a shoe salesman or working in a 7-Eleven. "I had no idea my dad was thinking about these things [because] he had to put food on the table."

The result is that as their family's situation improved---moving to a nicer house and sending their kids to better schools---Asif saw only the positive outcomes of his parents' risks. Doesn't it seem natural that he would simply believe that his own entrepreneurial ventures would also eventually work out, too?

Jon and Asif also had the experience of graduating from a top business school. They both insist that's not a prerequisite to success, and we hope we've proven that over the course of this book. But still, Jon said, "a great experience from business school was really about the socialization, learning that great entrepreneurs came from backgrounds just like you. And also a dose of brainwashing that you in fact really are worthy."

(We hope you've learned the same kinds of lessons from *Breakthrough Entrepreneurship,* at just a fraction of the cost!)

Once people are oriented to expect to achieve, Asif believes it's just a matter of degree. "There's a tremendous amount of luck that determines *how* successful you'll be," he told us, "but if you're oriented to be the sort of person who's proactive and learns to manage your fear, I think you're going to be successful whether you want to be a lawyer or a businessman or whatever. Just the attitude breeds success. I don't think being lucky brings success, it just influences the magnitude."

Eschew the track

Our educational system encourages people to track themselves. There's a balance to be struck here between offering students a legitimate probability of return on their educational investments and giving them the confidence and freedom they need to dare mighty things. From a larger point of view, though, why do we teach kids to follow tracks and rules, and suggest that you achieve by checking boxes and following a script---only to turn them loose on a society and a workplace that doesn't have any such rules?

If you've already graduated from college or graduate school, think of the rush you probably saw your peers engage in as commencement day approached. For many reasons---financial necessity, of course, but also social pressure---people flock to compete with one another for the same jobs, graduate schools, and other programs. College students who never had any interest in becoming teachers find themselves lining up to join Teach For America. Fledgling lawyers who started law school swearing they'd advocate professionally for the environment end up fighting for interviews with high-paying law firms. Business students and engineers who insist they wanted to start their own companies spend hundreds of hours angling to land jobs at consulting firms and banks. Opting out of that mad rush takes guts, but it can be the same kind of intestinal fortitude that enables to you take larger leaps of faith as an entrepreneur.

LEARNING TO MANAGE FEAR

Don't confuse faith with lack of fear. In fact, fear can be a necessary, even positive, component of entrepreneurship. It can stop you from taking audacious risks, sure---but it can also stop you from taking dumb risks.

"The key to overcoming fear is to break up the daunting tasks into small steps," says Jon.

At the very start of SupplierMarket, when he and Asif had tentatively settled on the general business idea, Jon put together a giant Gantt chart that took up an entire wall. On it, he broke down the steps of starting and building SupplierMarket into every tangible milestone they needed to achieve over the next 12 months. It covered everything from testing the idea early to building the team, gathering resources, leading and managing---and ultimately the step-by-step process of either going public or selling the whole thing. It might have seemed overwhelming to say, sitting in that apartment on Day One, that they planned to go public in a year. But breaking each step down made it all seem possible---although certainly not easy! And amazingly enough, even with all the unknowns and volatility of a new venture, Jon and Asif beat their original plan by a few days.

Fear never goes away completely, but you can also learn to channel your fears and use them as motivating tools instead of an excuse for inaction.

"I still get scared," said Asif. When he started his second and third companies, he was afraid he'd fail and "prove" that his earlier success had been a fluke. But he plays that fear against the expectation of all the great things that can happen---but only if he tries. "What's important is the ability to manage fear and the ability to deserve to be there. The way I do that is, first, recognize it. Ask yourself, 'Why I am afraid?' Go to the worst place first."

At the end of the day, if you're the kind of person who picked up and read this book, we can make a few predictions about you. Almost regardless of what you do or don't do, you're not going to starve. You're probably never going to have to worry seriously about whether you have basic necessities like a roof over your head. As long as you strive to behave ethically and honestly, as long as you don't become so prideful that you refuse to ask for help if you need it, and barring some unforeseen, uncontrollable catastrophe, you're probably going to live your entire life with a level of comfort that would be the envy of the vast majority of the world's people.

So why are we so fearful? It turns out that we're hard-wired for fear. From a neuroscience perspective, it's as if our brains are still running an operating system from back in the caveman days, when people had to worry about things like running out of meat or becoming a light summer supper for wild animals. When the brain's fear system kicks in, exploration and risk-taking are automatically set to shut off. As Gregory Burns, director of the Center for Neuropolicy at Emory University puts it, "No good can come from this type of decision-making. Fear prompts retreat. It is the antipode to progress. Just when we need new ideas most, everyone is seized up in fear, trying to prevent losing what we have left."

The solution, according to the neuroscientists among us, is not to be a fear monger---and, perhaps, to follow a few practical strategies. You wouldn't stop wearing a seatbelt just because you believe in an afterlife. So even if you embrace the attitude of entrepreneurial inevitability, minimize the downside, and cushion the fall in case it does happen.

LOWER YOUR OVERHEAD

It's striking how many very wealthy and successful entrepreneurs spend much less than they have and live far below their means. Warren Buffet is worth $45 billion and still famously lives in the same house he bought in 1958 for \$31,500. Once you have a roof over your head and your family's basic nutrition, health, education, and transportation needs provided for, every additional dollar you spend brings vastly diminished returns in terms of increasing your well-being.

Certainly, celebrate your wins. You don't need to live an austere life. But as an entrepreneur, be a producer in our society. Don't stab yourself in the back by becoming too much of a consumer, instead. Trust us, a BMW is nice, but in no way brings lasting happiness.

What about student loans? All things being equal, avoid them. At the very least, you want to ensure that if you're borrowing money for higher education there's a strong likelihood that you'll be able to increase your income sufficiently in a reasonably short period of time to pay them off. If you already have sizeable loans, they can be managed. Refinance them over 30 years, and drive a five-year-old Toyota. You don't need granite counter-tops, all the latest gadgets, or the highest-fashion clothing.

HAVE MARKETABLE SKILLS TO FALL BACK ON

A colleague of ours agreed to pay for his kids' college education, on the condition that they also learned a trade. His reasoning was that if they graduated and found themselves without a well-thought-through career path, they'd be much more confident and better-positioned if they also knew how to put up drywall, fix diesel engines, or work as an electrician's apprentice. They wouldn't have to rush to take some $20,000-a-year job they didn't much like anyway, and they'd likely be much happier as a result.

If you're still getting your basic education---say, through the undergraduate level---make sure to take at least a few courses geared directly toward practical moneymaking opportunities. That means making sure you take a couple of key computer science or hard science courses. If you're a professional planning to switch careers, maybe it makes sense to pay the few hundred dollars it costs to keep your annual professional licenses current and your continuing education up to date. If your entrepreneurial ship starts sinking you might be very glad to have a lifeboat waiting.

NURTURE YOUR NETWORK

They say that banks only lend money when you don't need it, so you should always acquire cash on favorable terms when you can. The same thing applies to your professional network. Do small favors for others. If you hear of a colleague looking to fill a position, for example, spend a few minutes thinking about who you know who might be a great fit, and make referrals. If your business doesn't work out and you need to find work, it's a lot easier to do so when the people you're asking for help know you as someone who goes out of your way to help others.

Likewise, if you plan to leave a job in order to start a new venture, make sure that you manage your exits. This isn't the time to declare victory and make some Howard Beale speech about how you never liked where you worked to begin with. Instead, be gracious, reflect on all the positive things you've learned and done, and preserve your relationships. You never know when you might be glad that you did.

FIND VALIDATION

Most of the impetus to believe that we can accomplish great things has to come from within. That said, it's striking how many successful people both in entrepreneurship and other fields talk about simple, fateful moments where others validated their ambitions and cemented their beliefs.

Jon and Asif were finalists in the Harvard Business School business plan competition, which both encouraged them and gave them credibility to outsiders. But for Jon, the bigger kind of external validation was simply to have investors and customers support their idea. Even in the earliest days when they tested their idea, Asif and Jon found that manufacturers were willing to sign up and even invest in the nascent venture. Later, on the first day the website was up and running, hundreds of suppliers signed up, completely overwhelming the servers.

We see these moments over and over in entrepreneurs' personal histories. In 1891, Henry Ford, then 27, met Thomas Edison, who was twenty years his senior. When Edison learned that Ford was working on a gasoline-powered car, Edison banged his fist in excitement.

"Young man, that's the thing!" Edison exclaimed.

Ford later wrote that Edison's brief words of encouragement had a huge impact on him: "All at once and out of a clear sky, the greatest inventive genius in the world had given me complete approval."

We could write an entire book just about these kinds of moments---for entrepreneurs and just about every person we've known who has achieved exceptional success in any field. Reporter and author Bob Woodward recalls the impact when the legendary editor of *The Washington Post*, Ben Bradlee, offered him a few words of encouragement a year or so before he broke the story of the Watergate scandal. Oprah Winfrey talks about what a confidence-booster it was when she was just a local talk show host and star-making producer Quincy Jones suggested that she should play a key role in the movie *The Color Purple*.

Most important for our purposes are that the validation comes from someone the aspiring person views as admirable and credible, and that the validation comes *after* the aspiring person has already taken steps toward his or her goal. You want to believe that the person validating your efforts knows what he's talking about---but also that you do, too.

As an aspiring entrepreneur, you want the chance to know these kinds of validating people when their impact on you will be greatest. So, plan ahead. Be outgoing and inquisitive, and make an effort to meet the people you respect in person. Join entrepreneurship groups. Attend conferences. Learn what is new. Your goal is to surround yourself with smart, enthusiastic people---and to build a support system of other people who strive to be exceptional.

Moreover, if you can, work for proven entrepreneurs.

"I don't think you go to the big companies," advised Asif. "I think you go to the companies where you see a leader you can learn from. Most of the people I've hired around here want to be an entrepreneur someday. When it comes to helping outsiders, I have a rule: Call three times, and you'll get me on the phone. Call five times, you'll get a meeting." (Note that with the publication of this book the thresholds for phone calls and meetings with Asif will probably increase a bit.) "I think entrepreneurs actually respect the people who pursue, and they will help them."

IN BUSINESS, MONEY TALKS

For an entrepreneur, perhaps the best kind of validation can come from customers or other key stakeholders. At age 25, Bill Gates got one of the most important validations he ever could have when he landed the deal to provide IBM's first-ever operating system. Steve Jobs and Steve Wozniak talk about how validating it was to realize in July 1976 that people were willing to pay them the somewhat odd price of $666.66 for their Apple I computer. We've heard entrepreneurs tell us that it was the supportive comment of an investor, a founder they respected, a teacher or mentor, or even a new employee that suddenly made them believe, wholeheartedly, that they were going to succeed.

FOLLOW THE FRAMEWORK

Finally, don't forget that the key aspect to believing you can do this is actually being able to. That's the whole point of the framework. When Jon sat in the Sequoia Capital conference room with his sweaty palms, what restored his expectations? It was the knowledge that he and Asif had prepared themselves flawlessly to be in that room. They'd brainstormed a great idea. They'd tested it thoroughly. They understood their value proposition, and they had constantly sought to enhance it. They'd recruited key stakeholders and hired some of the best possible people. They'd followed every step to obtain credibility and they'd already begun leading in an insightful, assertive style.

In short, they followed a well-thought-out, replicable process. And it worked.

THE BIG PICTURE

Our first four modules are the most important from a technical standpoint, but these last two modules are most crucial from a holistic point of view. Equipped with all the tools you need to succeed as an entrepreneur, you still need to be willing to use them. Throughout this book we've explored and learned from the examples of some fantastic entrepreneurs. But here's the surprise twist at the end. They're not the central characters. You are.

There are many reasons why people don't believe they are entitled to pursue and achieve greatness. All of them are illusions.

You are entitled to succeed, but you have to train yourself to believe that you will do so. We suppose some entrepreneurs believe this naturally, or they convince themselves with sheer drive and willpower. Honestly, though, that seems like an awful lot of work and it's not necessarily a replicable strategy. Instead, we think it makes more sense to plan ahead and put in place the supports you'll need along the way.

If you've ever run a long-distance race, you know that the organizers usually set up water stations every two or three miles along the way. They don't insist that running dehydrated be part of the competition; they do what they can to ensure that the runners are set up for success. So do the same thing as an entrepreneur. Prepare yourself for the full race. Minimize your overhead. Reduce your exposure. Confront your fears. Seek out peers and mentors. Set up metaphorical support stations before you need them.

Any giant goal can seem overwhelming, so break up the things you'll have to achieve as an entrepreneur into small steps. How do you do that? You've got the roadmap in your hands.

CONCLUSION

> "Do the difficult things while they are easy and do the great
> things while they are small. A journey of a thousand miles
> must begin with a single step."
>
> -Lao Tzu

A ROADMAP FOR SUCCESS

We hope this book has inspired you and guided you, and that you're excited to try your hand at launching the best new venture you can imagine. Before you do, however, we suggest two things.

First, go back and reread Module 1. Do the steps Robin Chase took make more sense to you now? Do you understand how her actions fit the framework we've discussed? Can you see how she identified customer pain, calculated a value proposition, and figured out her total addressable market? Do you appreciate how she built credibility, marshaled the needed resources, and employed an assertive leadership style as she launched her new venture?

Think hard about how you will follow those steps in your new enterprise. You know the framework, the distilled "how-to" from all the other entrepreneurs we've interviewed and studied. Think about how these people served their customers, created hundreds of billions of dollars of value, and changed the world. Force yourself to ask the same kinds of questions they asked, and you will tremendously increase your odds of success.

Second, once you've identified a promising idea, and after you've tested the heck out of it, pull out pen and paper. It's time to map out your action plan.

You're now going to break your entrepreneurial journey up into hundreds of little pieces. Figure out what you want to have achieved a month from today, a year from today, and two years from today. Maybe you want to have tested your prototype product with 50 customers. Maybe you want to have sold your product to your first 500 paying customers. Maybe you want to be filing for an initial public offering. Whatever it is, pick your end date and mark it.

Next, what milestones will you need to reach along the way? Will you need to revise your product based upon customer feedback? Build credibility with stakeholders? Hire employees? Figure out when you plan to have achieved each milestone in order to reach the ultimate goal, and mark those dates as well.

Now, determine the specific actions and resources you'll need in order to reach those milestones and detail them, too. Repeat the process yet again, breaking down the smaller actions into even more detailed tasks, and marking those dates.

Keep it up until you have a yearlong plan in which virtually every day contains a goal. Often, you may have more than one goal on a particular day. That's fine. You should be able to look at just about any date, whether it's three or six months down the road, and say, *by then we should have sold our product to 100 customers*, or else, *by this date, we should have upgraded our equipment so we can double our output.*

You may need to revise your calendar as you learn and progress. Perhaps you will realize you need to adjust your value proposition. Maybe you'll find previously unidentified business or technical risks, or recognize that you need other people or resources you weren't counting on.   Think about the things you've learned, focusing especially on the key questions we've been asking throughout. How will you continually test your ideas? What's your value proposition and total addressable market? What customer pain are you solving? How will you find your first five customers?

When you've got this complete, congratulations. You have built your own personal, actionable roadmap that you can follow to launch your new venture.

Starting a new company can seem overwhelming at first, no matter how badly you might want to do it. But if you break it down like this and follow each individual step, it suddenly seems a lot more manageable. You don't start the next Google by renting a garage and buying a bunch of computers. You start it by becoming obsessed with solving worthy problems, teaming up with the right people, and accessing the right resources.

All of which brings us to the final, most important conceptual point. You've seen the circumstances in which most of the entrepreneurs we talked about in this book began. Few of them had tremendous wealth at the outset. That's okay, of course, because entrepreneurship is *the pursuit of opportunity without regard to resources currently controlled.*

It hardly matters if you have limited money, power, or status. In fact, you may be better off in the long run if you don't have too many resources to start with. The entire point of entrepreneurship is to convince other institutions and people who *do* have resources to let you use them. Whether it's the capital you want to get from investors, the time and expertise you hope to get from employees, and especially the cold, hard cash that you want your customers to give you, your job---your calling---is to dream up better uses for other peoples' resources.

What do you call the result when enough people set their sights on entrepreneurship, come up with better uses resources, and implement a great plan for innovation? Creative destruction.

Professor Schumpeter recognized that the system works, paradoxically, only when the mavericks among us insist on bucking it. The world depends on original thinkers like you for its advancement. Understand, believe, disrupt, and succeed.

Over the next year, roughly seven million Americans will try to become entrepreneurs. But only a tiny percentage of their new ventures will survive, and an even smaller number will become extraordinary. Which group are you going to be a part of?

We're all pulling for you. But more importantly, as the swashbuckling economist recognized, we're all counting on you, too.

REFERENCES AND SOURCES

The backbone of *Breakthrough Entrepreneurship* consists of the framework for entrepreneurship that Jon Burgstone developed to better succeed at his own entrepreneurial ventures. He currently teaches the framework to students at the University of California, Berkeley, many of whom have used it to launch their own new businesses.

The muscle on those bones comes from the research and interviews we've done with some of the world's most successful entrepreneurs. This book would not exist if it were not for the generous gifts of time that so many founders shared with us. In almost all cases, they seemed to be motivated primarily by a desire to help others succeed.

We used a few other sources as well, and the following notes provide a bit more background on where we found the facts and assertions behind many of stories you've read within these pages.

MODULE I

The story of Zipcar is derived first and foremost from the authors' interviews with founder Robin Chase. Additional sources and background information on her story and contemporaneous data on Zipcar were derived from SEC filings and news articles. Robin Chase spoke for the first time at TED, as referenced in the module, in 2007, and she was named one of *Time* magazine's 100 most influential people in the world in April 2009. Her quote describing Zipcar's model is from an interview with Jacob Gordon of *Treehugger Radio* in June 2009, which can be found at www.treehugger.com. It's worth noting as well that Chase's story was documented in a Harvard Business School case. Cases like these can be great sources of inspiration and strategy, although be advised that they often adjust details to protect privacy or sharpen the teaching points.

Economist Joseph Schumpeter's legacy was put into perspective most completely by author Thomas K. McCraw in his acclaimed 2007 book, *Prophet of Innovation* (Belknap Press of Harvard University). If you can get through it, Schumpeter himself reduced his ideas on creative destruction to writing in his book, *Capitalism, Socialism, and Democracy* (1947).

MODULE 2

Author interviews with Boston Beer Company founder Jim Koch form the background of this module, along with several useful articles. If you'd like a bit more detail, we'd say to start with "Revolutionizing American Beer," by David Kesmodel, in the April 19, 2010 edition of *The Wall Street Journal*. For the record, Boston Beer Co. reached its status as the largest U.S.-owned beer maker only after Anheuser-Busch was purchased by Belgian conglomerate InBev (now known as Anheuser-Busch InBev), Miller Brewing Co. was purchased by London-based South African Breweries (now known as SAB Miller) and Coors was purchased by the Canadian brewer Molson (now known as Molson Coors Brewing Company).

The Innovator's Dilemma, by Harvard Business School Professor Clayton M. Christensen (Harvard Business School Press, 1997) is the book to read if you want to understand innovation and feature-creep. We first learned about John Osher, featured in the business example in this module, from the Harvard Business School case about his company, and we verified details and got more color from him in a series of email interviews.

MODULE 3

The authors' interview with Peter Thiel, who was the founder of PayPal and later the first significant investor in Facebook, was the most important source for our understanding of the insights he garnered while starting PayPal and his other ventures. (According to *Forbes*, Thiel was the 365th wealthiest individual in 2011, with a net worth of $1.5 billion, so his insights are likely worth paying attention to.) We also consulted numerous contemporaneous articles and interviews to get the facts surrounding PayPal's early years, including Eric M. Jackson's book, *The PayPal Wars* (World Ahead Publishing, 2004). The quote and story about how PayPal added the ability to transfer money with just an email address comes from Jackson's book as well.

The business example citing Hansen Industries stems in part from the personal experience of Hansen's president and founder, who is also the grandfather of coauthor Jon Burgstone. Details about the development, growth, and different markets targeted by RollerBlade USA were covered in many different articles from the 1980s and 1990s, and can be found on the company's website at www.rollerblade.com. Finally, we cited AOL Huffington Post Media Group as an example of an interesting value proposition for a media company. It's worth noting that the jury is still out, post-merger, as to whether the new company will be able to capture enough value to warrant the high purchase price.

MODULE 4

For years Professor Bill Sahlman of Harvard Business school has taught and advocated for entrepreneurs to obtain maximum information for minimum cost. Many are indebted to him for his sound wisdom and guidance.

Robin Wolaner, the founder Robin Wolaner, the founder of *Parenting* magazine, was kind enough to sit for an interview with us. We learned the background of her story from a Harvard Business School case about her, although again, while HBS cases are great learning tools, they sometimes include incorrect details. We verified key details of the story with Wolaner, and also through various news and magazine articles. The story of the would-be gourmet chocolatiers is true, but we changed some details due to privacy concerns.

MODULE 5

The primary source for the story of the development of B/E Aerospace was the authors' lengthy interview with the company's founder, Amin Khoury. Additional information can be found in various magazine articles and FAA reports. Michael Porter of Harvard Business School has written extensively on his Porter's Five Forces framework, beginning with *How Competitive Forces Shape Strategy*, a March/April 1979 article in the Harvard Business Review.

Craig McCaw's story about founding Cingular One and Nextel is told in several places, including articles going back as far as "The Wireless Wizard of Oz," by Jeffrey S. Young, in the June 22, 1998 edition of *Forbes*. For additional examination of management practices, we recommend especially the work of the late W. Edwards Deming (for example, his books including *Some Theory of Sampling* and *The New Economics*) and Peter F. Drucker (including *The Effective Executive, The Five Most Important Questions*, and *The Essential Drucker*).

Finally, the lessons of Tim Mott's experience in founding All Covered were derived primarily from the authors' interview with him.

MODULE 6

Jon Burgstone interviewed John Scharffenberger about how he built his companies during their memorable, tofu-infused walk through Berkeley, California. Other sources for this segment on how to build credibility included his interviews with *Inc.* (May 1, 2009) and *Ethicurean* (June 20, 2010).

To read more deeply into Robert Cialdini's work on persuasion and influence, begin with his book, *Influence: The Psychology of Persuasion.*

The business example of Rent the Runway was based on news reports and on the authors' interviews with cofounders Jennifer Hyman and Jenny Fleiss.

MODULE 7

We're told that Google CEO Larry Page allocates just 10 hours per year for media interviews. As a result, our account of the founding of Google relied heavily on the 2005 book *The Google Story*, by David Vise and Mark Malseed. Additionally, our account was influenced by an interview with the company's founding board member, Ram Shriram.

Other research that contributed to this chapter include the authors' interviews with entrepreneurs In Sik Rhee and Matt Szulik.

The SEC criteria for accredited investors that we mentioned are a bit more complicated than simply how much an individual makes. You can find them spelled out in Rule 501 of Regulation D, the section of the securities code in which they're contained. Finally, if you have any doubt that intellectual property fights benefit law firms more than any of the parties, check out the following article about the Bratz case:

MGA Defends $108 Million Fee Award in Bratz Fight, Documents Show, from the July 13, 2011 issue of The National Law Journal.

MODULE 8

Sam Walton, unfortunately, is no longer with us. However, his 1993 book, *Made in America,* provides great insight into how he developed his leadership style and what it was about it that enabled him to build Wal-Mart into the world's largest retailer. The story of the new company employee learning the hard way that Wal-Mart employees double up in motel rooms is a composite of many similar ones we've heard over the years.

We interviewed Kara Swisher, the founder of AllThingsD, for her insights on the styles of leadership that benefit great entrepreneurial companies. The example of a firm that developed its own version of Sam Walton's Saturday meetings comes from the New York-based career company, The Ladders, whose founder, Marc Cenedella, we interviewed. The details of Charles Ferguson's experience at Vermeer Technologies are derived from author interviews, and in one instance from the HBS case about his company. Finally, we recommend the work of Belen Villalonga and Raphael Amit, of Harvard Business School and the Wharton School at the University of Pennsylvania respectively ("How Do Family Ownership, Control, and Management Affect Firm Value?" in *The Journal of Financial Economics,* 2006), and especially Harvard Professor John Kotter's book, *Leading Change* (Harvard Business School Press 1996).

MODULE 9

Wendy Kopp's experience in starting Teach For America is recounted in detail in her book, *One Day All Children* (Public Affairs 2003), and we were also assisted in recounting her story in a series of email interviews with her via TFA's spokesperson. The organization's latest growth is chronicled in "A Chosen Few are Teaching for America," by Michael Winerip in the July 12, 2010 edition of *The New York Times*.

Darian Shirazi was one of Jon Burgstone's students at the University of California, Berkeley, and the authors interviewed him and Rev. William Swing for their stories. Burgstone was at the Young Presidents Organization meeting described in this module, although the names have been changed for privacy reasons. The estimate of the threshold beyond which wealth no longer provides additional happiness comes from an article by economists Angus Dean and Daniel Kahneman, "High Income Improves Evaluation of Life but not Emotional Well-being," in *Proceedings of the National Academy of Sciences* (September 6, 2010). Finally, we recommend the work of Martin Seligman for those interested to learn more about engineering happiness, including his books, *Flourish* (Free Press, 2011), and *Authentic Happiness* (Free Press, 2002).

MODULE 10

Many of the scenes and lessons of Module 10 come from the personal experience of coauthor Jon Burgstone. We also pushed hard to develop how he and cofounder Asif Satchu raised their expectations to unusual heights during a formal interview and give-and-take session with Satchu.

We also recommend reading some of Gregory Berns' work on the neuroscience of fear, such as his book, *Iconoclast* (Harvard Business School Press, 2008).

ACKNOWLEDGEMENTS

JON BURGSTONE:

We wrote this book to help give you a head start on launching a successful new venture. Along my journey, I have learned much from my interactions with the following people. For the glorious, the good, the bad, and the ugly, I offer my thanks to: Louis Hansen, Brad Loftus, Asif Satchu, Jay Light, Bill Sahlman, Mike Roberts, Ken Morse, Marco Iansiti, Tom Eisenmann, Charles Ferguson, Murray MacKenzie, Stacey Lawson, Ravi Mohan, Bob Barrett, Tim Connors, Mike Moritz, John Raguin, Reza Satchu, Peter Lamm, Keith Higgins, Mark Lipschultz, Henry Kravis and Brian Bethers. Lee Schruben, Ken Goldberg, Ikhlaq Sidhu, David Dornfeld, Ilan Adler, Richard Newton, Michael Marks, Jim Davidson, Tom Byers, and Ray Bingham. James Rembert, Glenn Fugitt, Randy Kroszner, Peter Thiel, Chris Rupright, Bart Stephens, and Warren Buffett. Darian Shirazi, Jeremy Schiff, Neil Warren, Heston Liebowitz, and Sharam Shirazi. I'd also like to thank Tom Bruett, and my co-author, Bill Murphy Jr.

Bill Murphy Jr.:

I met Jon Burgstone for the first time in San Francisco while I was writing another book. I owe thanks first and foremost to him for sharing his insights, ideas, and inspiration, as well as proving that an engineer can be an outstanding writing partner. I'm also grateful to the hundreds of other fantastic entrepreneurs I've been fortunate to have interviewed and studied over the years. Most everything I've learned about entrepreneurship, I learned from them. This is an incomplete list, but I owe special thanks to: Marla Malcolm Beck, Marc Cenedella, Robin Chase, Andrew Farquharson, Kathy Korman Frey, James Currier, Anne Dwane, Joseph Lassiter, Stig Leschly, Sheila Lirio Marcelo, Rick Marini, Chris Michel, Farquan Nazeeri, Bo Shao, Howard Stevenson, Noam Wasserman, Robin Wolaner and Ed Zschau. As a writer, the list of people I owe debts of gratitude is even longer, but two among them stand out for their help on this project. To Evelyn Duffy and Meredith Simons, thank you.

ABOUT THE AUTHORS

Jon Burgstone teaches entrepreneurship at the University of California, Berkeley, where he was the Founding Faculty Chair at the University's Center for Entrepreneurship and Technology. Previously, Burgstone was CEO and cofounder of SupplierMarket, an Internet software firm serving global enterprises that was acquired by Ariba, Inc. for $1.1 billion. A graduate of Harvard Business School and an advisor to the Rock Center for Entrepreneurship at Harvard, Burgstone lives in San Francisco, where he is also Managing Director of a successful private investment partnership.

Bill Murphy Jr. is the author of *The Intelligent Entrepreneur* and has written or collaborated on three other bestselling nonfiction books. A former reporter for *The Washington Post*, he has written for *The Atlantic, Newsweek, Real Simple, Wealth,* and other publications. He lives in Washington, DC.

n can be obtained at www.ICGtesting.com

2

)02B/5/P

9 780983 961109